WITHDRAWN

THE LEGACY OF STEVE JOBS
APPLE THROUGH THE YEARS

Lincoln Public Library   DUPL

3 7496 00327575 4

The Legacy of Steve Jobs

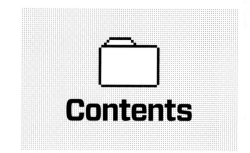

Contents

ON THE COVER: *PHOTOGRAPHS BY DIANA WALKER—CONTOUR BY GETTY IMAGES*

ICON ILLUSTRATIONS BY MICHAEL MYERS

APPLE CO-FOUNDER STEVE WOZNIAK AND JOBS AT JOBS' HOUSE IN 1981. **PHOTOGRAPH BY TED THAI—POLARIS**

FOREWORD

STEVE JOBS' LEGACY IS CLEAR: The most innovative businessman of our time. A cultural icon who revolutionized computing, telephony, movies, music, retailing, and product design. Underneath his relentless drive, Jobs has always had a single underlying passion—to show the world that he has the best understanding of how all of us would use technology. In the end he was proved right a billion times over, and his company Apple became one of the most successful enterprises on the planet.

How Jobs accomplished all this is less clear. His success is the sum total of thousands of assumptions, decisions, and roads taken. For the past three decades, *Fortune* has covered Steve's journey every step of the way. The stories contained in this new book from the editors of *Fortune* lay out in remarkable and unparalleled detail that this was no straight shot to success. Jobs, a man both loved and loathed, encountered all manner of intrigue, brick walls, and pitfalls before his ultimate vindication.

In these stories you will see Apple as the market share leader in PCs in the early 1980s, just as giant IBM rumbles onto the scene with its computers driven by the MS-DOS operating system, created by another brash young techie named Gates. Next comes Steve's banishment, then his return, and finally, the greatest accomplishments: his creation of the iPod, iTunes, the iPhone, and the Apple Store.

All these stories are the product of deep reporting. In many cases our writers spent hours interviewing Steve and delving into his mind. Veteran Apple watchers and award-winning journalists such as Brent Schlender, Adam Lashinsky, and Peter Elkind talked to dozens of Apple employees and insiders at length. The result is a singular journalistic collection that will leave you with a comprehensive picture of Steve Jobs and Apple, a picture that is complex in the making yet simple in its triumph.

Andy Serwer

MANAGING EDITOR, FORTUNE

↓ *STEVE JOBS AT HIS PALO ALTO HOME, DECEMBER 2004*

ODE TO A CONTRARIAN WHO CHANGED THE WORLD
BY MIGUEL HELFT

HERE'S TO THE CRAZY ONES. The misfits. The rebels. The troublemakers.

So began Apple's most memorable ad campaign, one that featured Albert Einstein and Martha Graham, Martin Luther King Jr. and Mahatma Gandhi, John Lennon and Pablo Picasso. It aired on television starting in 1997 and was plastered on the backs of magazines and on billboards everywhere. It urged us all to "Think different."

That such a lofty, high-minded campaign could be conceived without irony by a company that was on the verge of bankruptcy was pure chutzpah. It was pure Steve Jobs.

At the time it was impossible not to chuckle a bit when thinking that Jobs, undoubtedly and immodestly, saw a bit of himself in each of those giants.

But as it turns out, Jobs was right. He was a misfit and a rebel who dropped out of college to forge his own path. He was a troublemaker who picked battles with rivals and yelled at employees. He had the DNA of the artist, whose uncompromising aesthetic turned ordinary gadgets into objects of beauty. And as the celebrated ad campaign went on to say, he too was vilified and glorified, but he was impossible to ignore. At times, he was dismissed as crazy, yet he was a genius. He thought he could change the world, and he did.

Jobs is not the only strong-willed contrarian to spring from Silicon Valley's culture of innovation. And he is not the only one who proved to be right. But he is the only one who did so again and again, each time jolting the course of technology history a quantum leap forward.

Jobs was right when he created the Apple II and insisted that computers could be sold to consumers. He was right when he unveiled the Macintosh and changed the way billions of people interacted with computers. He was right when he saw magic in a computer-animation unit of Lucasfilm, which became Pixar. And he was right when he opened the first Apple store in 2001.

Jobs was also on the money when he dragged a reluctant music industry into the Digital Age with the iPod, and when he told recording studios that their future was in selling music by the song through iTunes. He was never more right than when he believed he could lead the mobile-computing revolution with the iPhone. Apple's most successful product ever, the iPhone battered giants like RIM and Nokia. And who would argue that Jobs was wrong when he brushed aside those who said consumers would not carry one more device and created the iPad? Overnight the iPad became a new, multibillion-dollar franchise that no competitor has been able to crack—and not for lack of trying.

But there were many times when Jobs' iconic status seemed far from assured. After dropping out of Reed College and traveling around India, Jobs and his high school friend Steve Wozniak started Apple Computer in the Jobs family garage. In 1977 the pair introduced the Apple II, the first computer to appeal to a mass audience. It was followed by two flops, the Apple III and the Lisa. It wasn't until 1984 that Jobs had another hit with the Macintosh. It was the first successful computer with a graphical user interface, inspired by an experimental computer Jobs had seen at Xerox PARC. Apple nevertheless struggled financially, and Jobs was sidelined by Apple's board after a series of clashes with John Sculley, the chief executive he had recruited from PepsiCo in 1983.

Jobs left Apple in 1985 and went on to found Next, a maker of computer workstations for the educational market. He also entered the film business in 1986, and after producing a string of blockbusters such as *Toy Story*, Jobs sold the studio, Pixar, to Disney for $7.4 billion. The deal turned Jobs into Disney's largest shareholder.

But the most remarkable phase of Jobs' career didn't start until 1997, shortly after a flailing Apple—at one point it was perilously close to insolvency—acquired Next and named Jobs interim CEO. (Next would become the foundation of the Mac OS X operating system.) He became permanent chief in 2000. Starting with the first iMac, Jobs created one blockbuster hit after another and completely rebuilt the struggling company into a model of management efficiency. With its stylish, revolutionary products, its far-flung, just-in-time supply chain, and its elegant stores, Apple became the most admired company in the world. And Jobs, who took a company in disarray and turned it into an enterprise worth more than $350 billion, became the most celebrated CEO of his generation, if not ever.

His success was clouded only by a controversy over the backdating of stock options, and by his battle with a rare form of pancreatic cancer, first diagnosed in 2003. Jobs appeared to recover after having surgery in mid-2004. But after losing weight steadily, he took a second medical leave in 2009 to undergo a liver transplant. During those years, Jobs and Apple's board were criticized for keeping most of the details of his medical condition secret from the public and from shareholders. In January 2011 an increasingly gaunt Jobs went on a third medical leave, and in August 2011 he resigned as CEO, handing the reins of Apple to Tim Cook, his top lieutenant for much of the past decade.

One of the few times Jobs spoke publicly about his illness was during a commencement address at Stanford in 2005. "Remembering that I'll be dead soon is the most important tool I've ever encountered to help me make the big choices in life," he told students. "Because almost everything—all external expectations, all pride, all fear of embarrassment or failure—these things just fall away in the face of death, leaving only what is truly important." He later went on, "Don't be trapped by dogma—which is living with the results of other people's thinking. Don't let the noise of others' opinions drown out your own inner voice. And most important, have the courage to follow your heart and intuition. They somehow already know what you truly want to become. Everything else is secondary." Trite? Not really. Not when you understand that Jobs lived by that credo, and in doing so, truly earned his place alongside Pablo Picasso, John Lennon, and the other rebels and misfits who changed the world.

Chapter One

WHAT MADE STEVE TICK

In these stories, published near the end of Steve Jobs' tenure as Apple's CEO, we went behind the scenes to find out how he applied his relentless drive for perfection, his sixth sense for what the consumer wanted, and his managerial iconoclasm to the company he built.

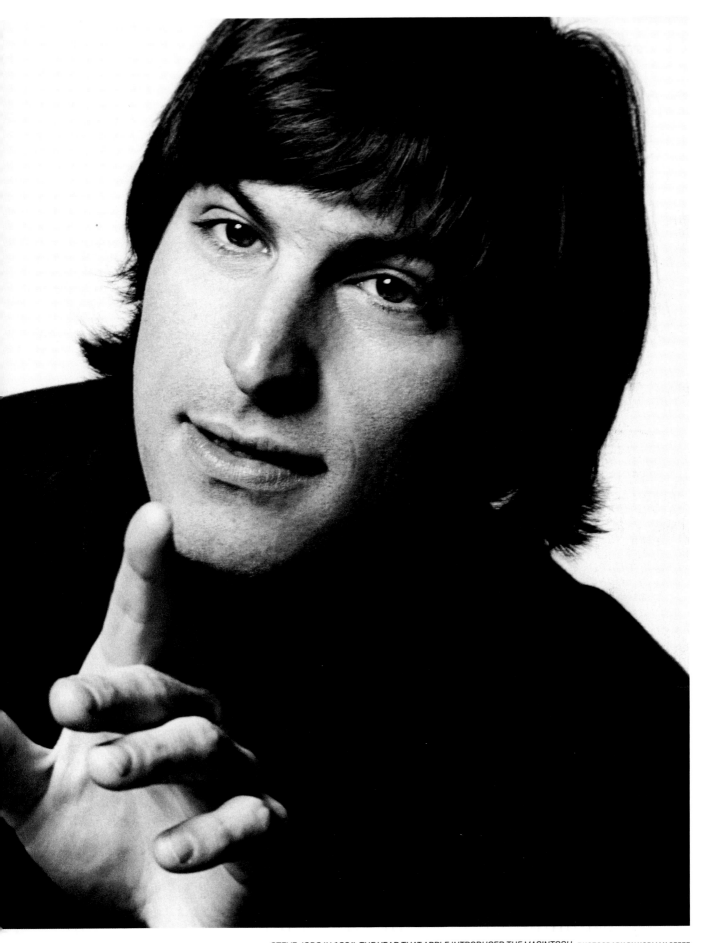

STEVE JOBS IN 1984, THE YEAR THAT APPLE INTRODUCED THE MACINTOSH **PHOTOGRAPH BY NORMAN SEEFF**

Apple Growers

In the past 10 years annual sales of Apple products have soared as its retail stores have proliferated.

COMPUTERS SOLD, UNITS

10 million

5

0

2000   2009*

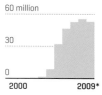

iPODS SOLD, UNITS

60 million

30

0

2000   2009*

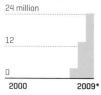

iPHONES SOLD, UNITS

24 million

12

0

2000   2009*

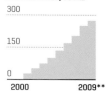

APPLE STORES, TOTAL

300

150

0

2000   2009**

*2009 ESTIMATE.
**THROUGH 10/22.

THE DECADE OF STEVE

HOW APPLE'S IMPERIOUS, BRILLIANT CEO TRANSFORMED AMERICAN BUSINESS.

BY ADAM LASHINSKY

TRUNK ARCHIVE; ARTWORK CREATED BY MEGAN CAPONETTO

H OW'S THIS for a gripping corporate story line: Youthful founder gets booted from his company in the 1980s, returns in the 1990s, and in the following decade survives two brushes with death, one securities-law scandal, an also-ran product lineup, and his own often unpleasant demeanor to become the dominant personality in four distinct industries, a billionaire many times over, and CEO of the most valuable company in Silicon Valley.

Sound too far-fetched to be true? Perhaps. Yet it happens to be the real-life story of Steve Jobs and his outsize impact on everything he touches.

The past decade in business belongs to Jobs. What makes that simple statement even more remarkable is that barely a year ago it seemed likely that any review of his accomplishments would be valedictory. But by deeds and accounts, Jobs is back. It's as if his signature "one more thing" line now applies to him as well. After a six-month leave of absence in the early part of 2009, during which he received a liver transplant, he is once again commanding a 34,000-strong corporate army that is as powerful, awe-inspiring, creative, secretive, bullying, arrogant—and yes, profitable—as at any time since he and his chum Steve Wozniak founded Apple in 1976.

Superlatives have attached themselves to Jobs since he was a young man. Now that he's 54, merely listing his achievements is sufficient explanation of why he's *Fortune*'s CEO of the Decade (though the superlatives continue). In the past 10 years alone, he has radically and lucratively reordered three markets—music, movies, and mobile telephones—and his impact on his original industry, computing, has only grown.

Remaking any one business is a career-defining achievement; four is unheard-of. Think about that for a moment. Henry Ford altered the course of the nascent auto industry. PanAm's Juan Trippe invented the global airline. Conrad Hilton internationalized American hospitality. In all instances, and many more like them, these entrepreneurs-turned-captains-of-industry defined a single market that had previously not been dominated by anyone. The industries that Jobs has turned topsy-turvy already existed when he focused on them.

He is the rare businessman with legitimate worldwide celebrity. (His quirks and predilections are such common knowledge that they were knowingly parodied on an episode of *The Simpsons*.) He pals around with U2's Bono. Consumers who have never picked up an annual report or even a business magazine gush about his design taste, his elegant retail stores, and his outside-the-box approach to advertising. ("Think different," indeed.) It's often noted that he's a showman, a born salesman, a magician who creates a famed reality-distortion field, a tyrannical perfectionist. It's totally accurate, of course, and the descriptions contribute to his legend.

Yet for all his hanging out with copywriters and industrial designers and musicians—and despite his anticorporate attire—make no mistake: Jobs is all about business. He may not pay attention to customer research, but he works slavishly to make products customers will buy. He's a visionary, but he's grounded in reality too, closely monitoring Apple's various operational and market metrics. He isn't motivated by money, says friend Larry Ellison, CEO of Oracle. Rather, Jobs is understandably driven by a visceral ardor for Apple, his first love (to which he returned after being spurned—proof that you can go home again) and the vehicle through which he can be both an arbiter of cool and a force for changing the world.

JUSTIN SULLIVAN—GETTY

The financial results have been nothing short of astounding—for Apple and for Jobs. The company was worth about $5 billion in 2000, just before Jobs unleashed Apple's groundbreaking "digital lifestyle" strategy, understood at the time by few critics. Today, at about $170 billion, Apple is slightly more valuable than Google. Its market share in personal computers was plummeting back then, and the cash drain was so severe that bankruptcy was a possibility. Now Apple has $34 billion in cash and marketable securities, surpassing the total market cap of rival Dell. Macintoshes make up 9% of the PC market in the U.S. today, but that share is increasingly beside the point. With 275 retail stores in nine countries, a 73% share of the U.S. MP3-player market, and the undisputed leadership position in innovation when it comes to mobile phones, Apple and its CEO are no one's idea of underdogs anymore. In 2006, Disney paid $7.5 billion to acquire Pixar, the computer-animation film studio Jobs had nurtured and controlled. Jobs, in turn, became a Disney director and the blue-chip company's largest shareholder. His net worth, solely based on his stakes in Apple and Disney, is about $5 billion. Other executives have had stellar decades, but none can compare to Steve's.

With Jobs back at the helm of his company, plenty of challenges lie ahead. Will the Goliath role suit him nearly as well as playing David clearly has? How will he respond to the competition he has awakened, particularly in smartphones, even as the personal computer fades in relative importance? Has he fashioned an organization that can succeed him? Can he possibly be as dominant in the decade to come as the one that is ending?

T HE "DECADE" OF STEVE actually began in 1997, when he returned to Apple after having been ousted a dozen years earlier. That was a year of triage, of a humbling investment from Microsoft, of paring Apple's product line to a bare minimum of four computers. By the following year Steve's regime had kicked into gear. Jobs completed the hiring of a new management team, which included several executives from his previous company, Next. Those top players would form the nucleus of the Jobs brain trust for nearly 10 years. Then came the first Macintosh after Jobs' return, the iMac, a breakthrough all-in-one computer and monitor that heralded Apple's return to health. The success of the pricey iMac, coupled with drastic cost cutting, allowed Jobs to build a cash cushion. By repairing Apple's balance sheet, he prepared the company for big investments to come, a shrewd business move if ever there was one.

Jobs laid the foundation for Apple's leap from stable to stratospheric when things looked darkest. In 2000, Apple missed its financial targets in a September earnings announcement, sending its stock price plummeting in subsequent months to the equivalent of $7 in today's prices. Yet Jobs by this time had set in motion the key elements of Apple's rejuvenation. Over the course of 2001, as global markets fell and the world headed into recession, Apple launched the iTunes music software (in January), the Mac OS X operating system (March), the first Apple retail stores (May), and the first iPod (November), a 5GB model that Apple bragged would hold 1,000 songs.

The market didn't catch on quickly to the significance of those events. iTunes was just music-playing software embedded into Macs and lacked an online store that sold music. The new operating system, though impressive, powered a niche product. The iPod was a snazzy MP3 player in an established market. As the company's stock languished, takeover rumors appeared from time to time. What was never reported was that Jobs seriously contemplated taking the company private with the help of newly formed buyout group Silver Lake Partners. An Apple buyout would have been the deal of the century, but according to people familiar with the talks, Jobs ultimately shut them down.

That was actually the second serious proposal to buy Apple. In 1997, Jobs' friend Ellison, later an Apple board member, lined up financing to take over the company on the assumption that Jobs would run it. In a recent interview Ellison said Jobs didn't like the idea of being "second-guessed" if it looked as if he'd returned simply to make money. "He explained to me that with the moral high ground, he thought he could make decisions more easily and more gracefully," says Ellison.

For those paying attention after Jobs' return, the CEO was telegraphing Apple's trajectory. "I would rather compete with Sony than compete in another product category with Microsoft," he told *Time* in early 2002. "We're the only company that owns the whole widget—the hardware, the software, and the operating system. We can take full responsibility for the user experience. We can do things that the other guy can't do." Jobs was convinced that the masses would turn to Apple, but only if he could speak directly to them—and not just to faithful Macintosh users, a club that included mainly artists and students. The strategy of building company-owned retail stores, so integral to Apple today, was derided at the time as a risky cash drain. "He did this with a nervous board," says Bill Campbell, a former Apple executive who went on to become chairman of Intuit and an Apple board member. "He knew that this is what customers wanted." What's striking looking back is how little there was to sell in the original Apple stores. Jobs knew how he'd fill them.

Jobs made it his business to know everything about Apple. "He's involved in details you wouldn't think a CEO would be involved in," says Ken Segall, a former Chiat/Day creative director who has worked with Apple on and off for years. Jobs commissioned the iconic "Think different" campaign, says Segall, well before any of Apple's new products were introduced—or even described to the ad team. "He'd say, 'The third word in the fourth paragraph isn't right. You might want to think about that one.'"

The rare pairing of micromanagement with big-picture vision is a Jobs hallmark. Early in his return to Apple, he recognized that gorgeous design was a differentiator for Apple in a computer industry gripped by the successful blandness of Dell, Microsoft, and Intel. "I cannot count the number of clients who have marched in and said, 'Give me the next iPod,'" writes Tim Brown, CEO of product-design consultant Ideo, in his new book *Change by Design*. "But it's probably close to the number of designers I've heard respond—under their breath—'Give me the next Steve Jobs.'"

Jobs also has a knack for pouncing at the right moment. The music industry had failed repeatedly to develop its own digital-music sales site before Apple came along with iTunes, which was by then prepared to become a store for buying music. Jobs cleverly made his pact with the record labels when iTunes worked only on Macs, which in 2002 had a personal-computing market share in the low single digits. Apple's humble position—before iTunes became compatible with Windows, expanding its potential market share to nearly all PCs—was a virtue. This made iTunes an experiment rather than a destructive paradigm shift. "I don't understand how Apple could ruin the record business in one year on Mac," said Doug Morris, the head of Universal Music, according to *Appetite for Self-Destruction*, a new book about the record industry's ills by *Rolling Stone* writer Steve Knopper. "Why shouldn't we try this?" Writes Knopper: "By the time Steve Jobs came around, he was the last resort. He was merely smart enough to know it. He played tough, but not any tougher than any lawyer for a major label who had negotiated an artist contract in recent decades."

A key Jobs business tool is his mastery of the message. He rehearses over and over every line he and others utter in public about Apple, which authorizes only a small number of executives to speak publicly on a given topic. Key to the Jobs approach is careful consideration of what he and Apple say—and don't say. Harvard professor David Yoffie estimated that in the months between announcing and selling the first iPhone in 2007, Apple received $400 million in free advertising by not making any public statements, thereby whipping the media into a frenzy. Jobs himself is careful to avoid overexposure, preferring to speak only when he has

JUSTIN SULLIVAN—GETTY

products to promote. He didn't disclose his 2004 cancer surgery until after it occurred, and then only in an employee e-mail that was strategically released to news outlets. Similarly, he told the world of his leave in another employee missive, with no additional comment from him or anyone else at Apple. Nobody in Jobs' sphere speaks without the permission of the company's media relations team, which reports directly to Jobs. Apple declined to make Jobs available for an interview for this article. It did bless the participation of some people in Apple's orbit to speak about him, while nixing requests for others.

The secrecy has rankled corporate governance experts, who insist the health of such an indispensable CEO warrants greater disclosure. Jobs was initially mum as well about a stock options backdating scandal that embroiled the company's former finance chief and general counsel. In an eventual SEC filing, Apple said Jobs was aware that the company had adjusted option grant dates so that the grants were more profitable for employees. Jobs apologized for the backdating, calling the episode "completely out of character for Apple."

Jobs manages the money, the message, the deals, the design, and more. Consider the case fairly made that the long-ago *enfant terrible* of the computer industry has built up impressive business chops and that his company is peerless. But if nothing else, his recent illness is a reminder that Steve Jobs is mortal. When he's gone, how long will his company thrive without him?

THIS PAST SEPTEMBER, when Steve Jobs made his triumphant return to the public eye, he thanked precisely one Apple executive by name: Tim Cook, Apple's chief operating officer. At an event to introduce a new line of iPods, Jobs first informed a crowd of journalists, analysts, and Apple developers that he now possessed the liver of a "twentysomething liver donor who had died in a car crash." Then he thanked Cook and the rest of the management team for "ably" running Apple in his absence. Cook, in turn, led a standing ovation for Jobs, his arms raised over his head from the front row of a San Francisco auditorium.

With Jobs back at work, the conversation has been postponed as to whether Cook, or anyone else, is prepared to fill Jobs' shoes. "At Apple the hierarchy is determined by who Steve calls," says a former Apple executive. "There's a lot of value in 'Steve said.' " Larry Ellison, a CEO known to dislike the topic of succession, says of his friend, "He's irreplaceable. He's built a fabulous brand. He's got a wealth of products. Whenever he leaves, I hope he retires in good health and

JOBS WITH DISNEY CEO BOB IGER AFER THE ENTERTAINMENT GIANT ANNOUNCED IT WAS BUYING PIXAR

he's sailing off in his yacht in the Mediterranean. But they're going to miss him terribly, because it's a consumer products company. The product cycle is so fast."

There are signs that Jobs has inculcated the troops enough to last awhile without him. "The organization has been thoroughly trained to think like Steve," says someone with contacts among the Apple executive team. "That's why the six months went so smoothly. People could envision, 'This is what Steve would do.' "

Jobs, in fact, inspires far beyond Apple. Larry Page and Sergey Brin recently told *The New Yorker* that Jobs is their hero. When Jeff Bezos released Amazon.com's smooth, shiny Kindle 2, the Jobs envy was obvious. Venture capitalist Marc Andreessen, who co-founded Netscape, says he often evokes Jobs in his advice to entrepreneurs. He says, "The threshold for the release of the first product should be, 'What would Steve Jobs do?' "

Looking out on the next decade, Jobs may well be asking himself a variation of that very question: After creating more than $150 billion in shareholder wealth, transforming movies, telecom, music, and computing (and profoundly influencing the worlds of retail and design), what should Steve Jobs do next? Given his penchant for secrecy and surprise and his proven brilliance, it's a fair bet that he'll let us know when he's good and ready.

Reporter associate: Doris Burke

PAUL SAKUMA—AP

The Legacy of Steve Jobs

Chapter One

ilovedust

Fortune
May 3,
2011

Apple
Profile

Stock
That Rocks

APPLE STOCK PRICE, MONTHLY

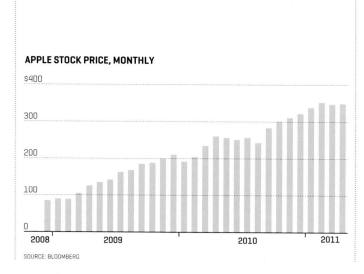

SOURCE: BLOOMBERG

RANK:
35

REVENUE:
$65.2 billion

PROFITS:
$14 billion

**TOTAL RETURN TO
INVESTORS IN 2010:**
53.1%

MARKET VALUE, 3/25/11:
$323.9 billion

The stock chart tells
the story of Apple's
ascent: Since January
2009, when CEO
Steve Jobs announced
the second of three
medical leaves of
absence, to April 2011,
shares have soared
310%. Some investors
contend that the stock,
which trades at less
than 17 times earnings,
is undervalued.

INSIDE APPLE
FROM STEVE JOBS DOWN TO THE JANITOR: HOW AMERICA'S MOST SUCCESSFUL—AND MOST SECRETIVE— BIG COMPANY REALLY WORKS.
BY ADAM LASHINSKY

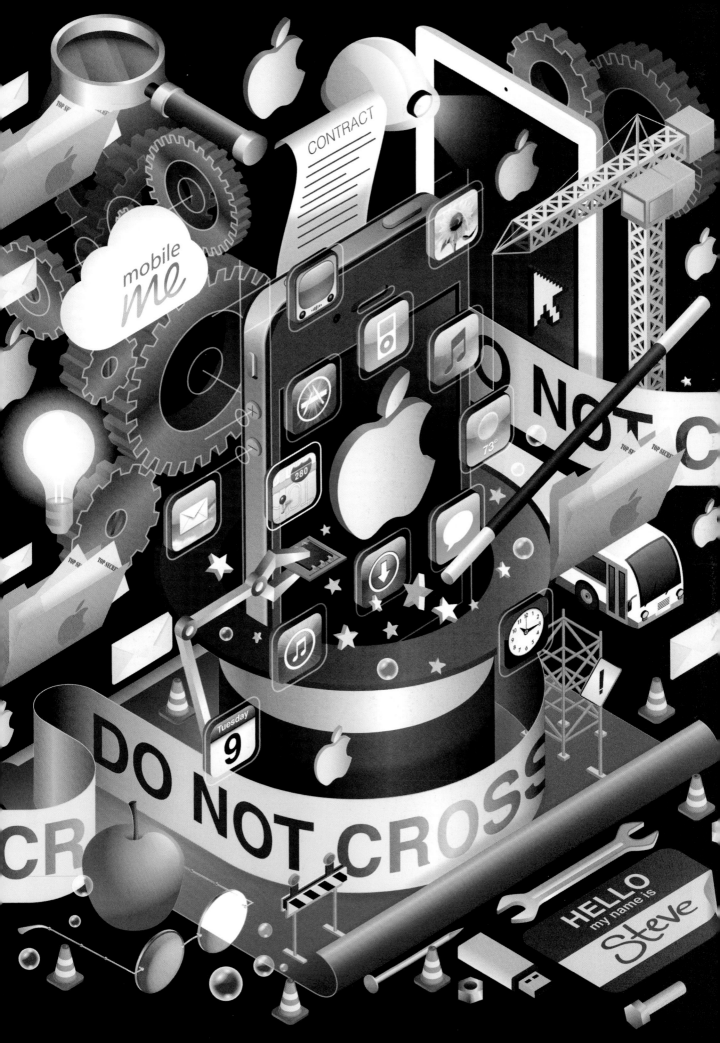

APPLE DOESN'T OFTEN FAIL, and when it does, it isn't a pretty sight at 1 Infinite Loop. In the summer of 2008, when Apple launched the first version of its iPhone that worked on third-generation mobile networks, it also debuted MobileMe, an e-mail system that was supposed to provide the seamless synchronization features that corporate users love about their BlackBerry smartphones. MobileMe was a dud. Users complained about lost e-mails, and syncing was spotty at best. Though reviewers gushed over the new iPhone, they panned the MobileMe service.

Steve Jobs doesn't tolerate duds. Shortly after the launch event, he summoned the MobileMe team, gathering them in the Town Hall auditorium in Building 4 of Apple's campus, the venue the company uses for intimate product unveilings for journalists. According to a participant in the meeting, Jobs walked in, clad in his trademark black mock turtleneck and blue jeans, clasped his hands together, and asked a simple question:

"Can anyone tell me what MobileMe is supposed to do?" Having received a satisfactory answer, he continued, "So why the fuck doesn't it do that?"

For the next half-hour Jobs berated the group. "You've tarnished Apple's reputation," he told them. "You should hate each other for having let each other down." The public humiliation particularly infuriated Jobs. Walt Mossberg, the influential *Wall Street Journal* gadget columnist, had panned MobileMe. "Mossberg, our friend, is no longer writing good things about us," Jobs said. On the spot, Jobs named a new executive to run the group.

Jobs' handling of the MobileMe debacle offers a rare glimpse of how Apple really operates. To Apple's legion of

ROBYN TWOMEY—CORBIS OUTLINE

admirers, the company is like a tech version of Wonka's factory, an enigmatic but enchanted place that produces wonderful items they can't get enough of. That characterization is true, but Apple also is a brutal and unforgiving place, where accountability is strictly enforced, decisions are swift, and communication is articulated clearly from the top. (After Jobs' tirade, much of the MobileMe team disbanded, and those left behind eventually turned MobileMe into the service Jobs demanded.)

Apple's ruthless corporate culture is just one piece of a mystery that virtually every business executive in the world would love to understand: How does Apple do it? How does a company with more than 50,000 employees and with annual revenue approaching $100 billion grow 60% a year? How does it churn out hit after hit? Those are questions Apple has no desire to answer. This past January, when a Wall Street analyst asked Tim Cook, Apple's low-key chief operating officer, how far out the company conducts long-term planning, Cook replied with an artful brushoff. "Well, that is a part of the magic of Apple," he said. "And I don't want to let anybody know our magic because I don't want anybody copying it."

Just because a magician doesn't want to reveal his tricks doesn't mean it's impossible to figure them out. *Fortune* conducted dozens of interviews over several months with former Apple employees and others in the Apple orbit to try to explain the phenomenon of life inside Apple. Few agreed to speak on the record; the fear of retribution persists for years. Once they get talking, however, the former Apple-ites paint a picture of a company that time and again thumbs its nose at modern corporate conventions in ways that let it behave more like a cutting-edge startup than the consumer electronics behemoth it is.

Whether Apple's startup ways are sustainable or the result of the sheer will of Steve Jobs is the great unknown in explaining how Apple works. Every conversation with insiders about Apple, even if it doesn't start out being about Jobs, eventually comes around to him. The creative process at Apple is one of constantly preparing someone—be it one's boss, one's boss's boss, or oneself—for a presentation to Jobs. He's a corporate dictator who makes every critical decision and oodles of seemingly noncritical calls too, from the design of the shuttle buses that ferry employees to and from San Francisco to what food will be served in the cafeteria.

But just as Jobs sees everything going on at the company, he's not blind to the fact that things will be radically different without him at the top. Jobs currently is on his third medical leave in seven years—he survived a rare form of pancreatic cancer and later received a liver transplant—and his absence

has only fueled the fascination with him. Jobs is still heavily involved in Apple, of course. He personally took charge of Apple's response to the recent Locationgate, for example, granting interviews to several news outlets to answer accusations that Apple is tracking the whereabouts of iPhone users. On a more strategic level, these days he's especially focused on institutionalizing his ways of doing business. His mission: to turn the traits that people most closely associate with Jobs— the attention to detail, the secrecy, the constant feedback—into processes that can ensure Apple's excellence far into the future.

S O EXALTED IS STEVE JOBS that often he is compared, metaphorically at least, to Jesus Christ. (Exhibit A: Alan Deutschman's revealing 11-year-old book, *The Second Coming of Steve Jobs*.) True to form, the shepherd to his Apple flock often teaches in parables. One such lesson could be called "The Difference Between the Janitor and the Vice President," and it's a sermon Jobs delivers every time an executive reaches the VP level. Jobs imagines his garbage regularly not being emptied in his office, and when he asks the janitor why, he gets an excuse: The locks have been changed, and the janitor doesn't have a key. This is an acceptable excuse coming from someone who empties trash bins for a living. The janitor gets to explain why something went wrong. Senior people do not. "When you're the janitor," Jobs has repeatedly told incoming VPs, "reasons matter." He continues: "Somewhere between the janitor and the CEO, reasons stop mattering." That "Rubicon," he has said, "is crossed when you become a VP." (Apple has about 70 vice presidents out of more than 25,000 non-retail-store employees.)

Jobs inculcates a culture of responsibility by hosting a series of weekly meetings that are the metronome that sets the beat for the entire company. On Mondays he meets with his executive management team to discuss results and strategy as well as to review nearly every important project in the company. On Wednesdays he holds a marketing and communications meeting. Simplicity breeds clarity, as Jobs himself explained in a 2008 interview with *Fortune*. "Every Monday we review the whole business," he said. "We look at every single product under development. I put out an agenda. Eighty percent is the same as it was the last week, and we just walk down it every single week. We don't have a lot of process at Apple, but that's one of the few things we do just to all stay on the same page." It's one thing when the leader describes the process. It's another thing altogether when the troops candidly parrot back the impact it has on them. "From a design perspective, having every junior-level designer getting

APPLE CEO AND CO-FOUNDER STEVE JOBS ON MARCH 2, 2011, EMERGED FROM A MEDICAL LEAVE OF ABSENCE TO INTRODUCE THE SECOND GENERATION OF THE IPAD.

direct executive-level feedback is killer," says Andrew Borovsky, a former Apple designer who now runs 80/20, a New York design shop. "On a regular basis you either get positive feedback or are told to stop doing stupid shit."

The accountability mindset extends down the ranks. At Apple there is never any confusion as to who is responsible for what. Internal Applespeak even has a name for it, the "DRI," or directly responsible individual. Often the DRI's name will appear on an agenda for a meeting, so everybody knows who is responsible. "Any effective meeting at Apple will have an action list," says a former employee. "Next to each action item will be the DRI." A common phrase heard around Apple when someone is trying to learn the right contact on a project: "Who's the DRI on that?"

Simplicity also is key to Apple's organizational structure. The org chart is deceptively straightforward, with none of the dotted-line or matrixed responsibilities popular elsewhere in the corporate world. There aren't any committees at Apple, the concept of general management is frowned on, and only one person, the chief financial officer, has a "P&L," or responsibility for costs and expenses that lead to profits or losses. It's a radical example of Apple's different course: Most companies view the P&L as the ultimate proof of a manager's accountability; Apple turns that dictum on its head by labeling P&L a distraction only the finance chief needs to consider. The result is a command-and-control structure where ideas are shared at the top—if not below. Jobs often contrasts Apple's approach with its competitors'. Sony, he has said, had too many divisions to create the iPod. Apple instead has functions. "It's not synergy that makes it work," is how one observer paraphrases Jobs' explanation of Apple's approach. "It's that we're a unified team."

For Apple the result is an ability to move nimbly, despite its size. "Constant course correction" is how one former executive refers to the approach. "If the executive team decides to change direction, it's instantaneous," this ex-Apple honcho says. "Everybody thinks it's a grand strategy. It's not." As an example, Apple's management has been known to change

its pricing 48 hours before a product launch. When it misses a seemingly obvious idea—such as not anticipating the need for an App Store to satisfy the third-party developers who wanted to create programs for the iPhone—it shifts gears quickly to grab the opportunity.

One of Apple's greatest strengths is its ability to focus on just a few things at a time, an entrepreneurial trait difficult to imagine at a corporation with a market value of $320 billion. Saying no at Apple is as important as saying yes. "Over and over Steve talks about the power of picking the things you don't do," says one recently departed executive. Obvious? Perhaps. Yet few companies of Apple's size—and very few of any size—are able to focus so well and for so long.

Jobs himself is the glue that holds this unique approach together. Yet his methods have produced an organization that mirrors his thoughts when—and this is important—Jobs isn't specifically involved. Says one former insider: "You can ask anyone in the company what Steve wants, and you'll get an answer, even if 90% of them have never met Steve."

THERE IS A SMALL GROUP at Apple that most certainly has met Steve Jobs. It's called the Top 100, and every year or so Jobs gathers these select few for an intense three-day strategy session at a proverbially secure, undisclosed location. Everything about this Top 100 meeting is shrouded in secrecy, starting with its very existence. Those tapped to attend are encouraged not to put the meeting on their calendars. Discussing their participation is a no-no, even internally. Attendees aren't allowed to drive themselves to the gathering. Instead they ride buses that depart from Apple's Cupertino, Calif., headquarters to places like the sumptuous Chaminade Resort & Spa in Santa Cruz, Calif., which satisfies two Jobs requirements: good food and no golf course. Apple goes so far as to have the meeting rooms swept for electronic bugs to stymie snooping competitors.

The Top 100 meeting is an important managerial tool for Jobs. He and his chief lieutenants use it to inform a supremely influential group about where Apple is headed. The elaborately staged event also gives Jobs an opportunity to share his grand vision with Apple's next generation of leaders. The Top 100 meeting is part strategic offsite, part legacy-building exercise.

Jobs generally kicks things off personally. Each session is as well crafted as the public product debuts for which the CEO is so famous. For presenters the career stakes are high, and the pressure is nerve-racking. "The Top 100 was a horrifying experience for 10 or so people," recalls one former

KIMIHIRO HOSHINO—AFP/GETTY

APPLE'S CORE

An unconventional org chart for an unconventional organization. CEO Jobs is at the center of it all.

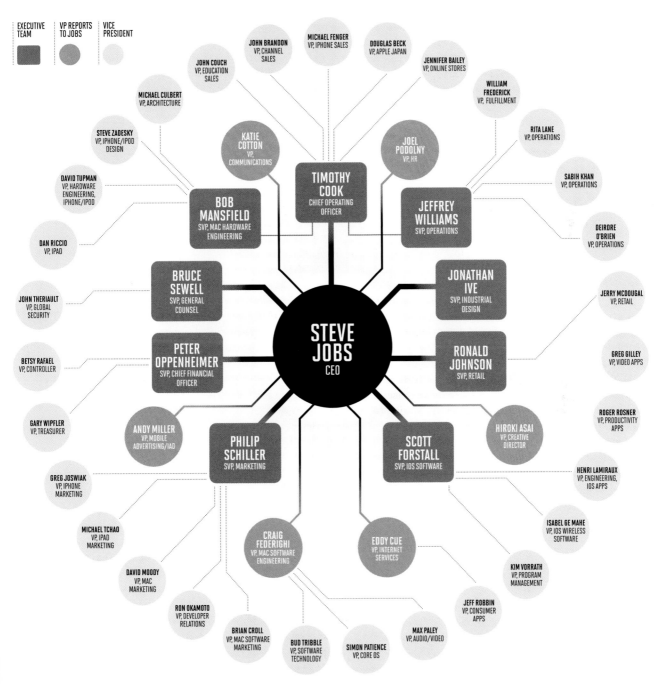

EXECUTIVE TEAM | **VP REPORTS TO JOBS** | **VICE PRESIDENT**

JOHN COUCH VP, EDUCATION SALES
JOHN BRANDON VP, CHANNEL SALES
MICHAEL FENGER VP, IPHONE SALES
DOUGLAS BECK VP, APPLE JAPAN
JENNIFER BAILEY VP, ONLINE STORES
MICHAEL CULBERT VP, ARCHITECTURE
WILLIAM FREDERICK VP, FULFILLMENT
STEVE ZADESKY VP, IPHONE/IPOD DESIGN
RITA LANE VP, OPERATIONS
KATIE COTTON VP, COMMUNICATIONS
JOEL PODOLNY VP, HR
DAVID TUPMAN VP, HARDWARE ENGINEERING, IPHONE/IPOD
SABIH KHAN VP, OPERATIONS
TIMOTHY COOK CHIEF OPERATING OFFICER
BOB MANSFIELD SVP, MAC HARDWARE ENGINEERING
JEFFREY WILLIAMS SVP, OPERATIONS
DAN RICCIO VP, IPAD
DEIRDRE O'BRIEN VP, OPERATIONS
BRUCE SEWELL SVP, GENERAL COUNSEL
JONATHAN IVE SVP, INDUSTRIAL DESIGN
JOHN THERIAULT VP, GLOBAL SECURITY
JERRY MCDOUGAL VP, RETAIL
STEVE JOBS CEO
PETER OPPENHEIMER SVP, CHIEF FINANCIAL OFFICER
RONALD JOHNSON SVP, RETAIL
GREG GILLEY VP, VIDEO APPS
BETSY RAFAEL VP, CONTROLLER
ROGER ROSNER VP, PRODUCTIVITY APPS
GARY WIPFLER VP, TREASURER
ANDY MILLER VP, MOBILE ADVERTISING/IAD
HIROKI ASAI VP, CREATIVE DIRECTOR
PHILIP SCHILLER SVP, MARKETING
SCOTT FORSTALL SVP, IOS SOFTWARE
GREG JOSWIAK VP, IPHONE MARKETING
HENRI LAMIRAUX VP, ENGINEERING, IOS APPS
MICHAEL TCHAO VP, IPAD MARKETING
ISABEL GE MAHE VP, IOS WIRELESS SOFTWARE
DAVID MOODY VP, MAC MARKETING
CRAIG FEDERIGHI VP, MAC SOFTWARE ENGINEERING
EDDY CUE VP, INTERNET SERVICES
KIM VORRATH VP, PROGRAM MANAGEMENT
RON OKAMOTO VP, DEVELOPER RELATIONS
JEFF ROBBIN VP, CONSUMER APPS
BRIAN CROLL VP, MAC SOFTWARE MARKETING
MAX PALEY VP, AUDIO/VIDEO
BUD TRIBBLE VP, SOFTWARE TECHNOLOGY
SIMON PATIENCE VP, CORE OS

No decision-maker at Apple is far removed from Steve Jobs. Through his tight-knit and largely long-serving executive team, Jobs quickly sees everything that goes on at the company. He also routinely reaches outside these inner and outer circles to collaborate on critical projects with key employees. This organization chart, which includes most but not all Apple executive officers, is based on *Fortune*'s reporting, in addition to some limited information Apple releases publicly.

INFOGRAPHIC: DAVID FOSTER

vice president who took the stage some years ago. "For the other 90 it's the best few days of their life." Jobs sometimes uses the occasion to unveil important initiatives. "I was at a Top 100 when Steve showed us the iPod," says Mike Janes, who worked at Apple from 1998 to 2003 and remains close to Apple executives. "Apart from a tiny group, no one knew anything about it."

To be selected for the Top 100 is to be anointed by Jobs, an honor not necessarily based on rank. Jobs referred to the group, but not the conclave, in an interview several years ago with *Fortune*. "My job is to work with sort of the Top 100 people," he said. "That doesn't mean they're all vice presidents. Some of them are just key individual contributors. So when a good idea comes ... part of my job is to move it around [and] ... get ideas moving among that group of 100 people." Privately Jobs has spoken even more strongly about the Top 100's importance. "If he had to recreate the company, these are the 100 people he'd bring along" is how one former Apple executive describes Jobs' characterization.

Though its name isn't to be uttered, the blessed nature of the gathering creates a caste system at Apple. Inclusion is by no means permanent. According to Jobs' whims, attendees can be bumped from one year to the next, and being kicked out of this exclusive club is humiliating. For those left behind in Cupertino, chattering begins as soon the chosen few have departed. "We'd tongue-in-cheek have a Bottom 100 lunch after we were done preparing the people who'd left," recalls one nonparticipant. Says another: "We weren't supposed to know where they were. But we all knew."

APPLE IS NOW 35 YEARS OLD, an extremely mature company by Silicon Valley standards, and there's a grownup atmosphere at headquarters: You won't find a lot of people dressed in board shorts and flip-flops, or zanily decorated cubicles. The vibe is the opposite of the jocularity that Google, with its wear-your-pajamas-to-work day and all-you-can-eat cafeterias, has fostered. There literally is no free lunch at Apple, though meals are subsidized and generally quite good.

Yet Apple also consciously tries to behave like a startup, most notably by putting small teams on crucial projects. To wit: Just two engineers wrote the code for converting Apple's Safari browser for the iPad, a massive undertaking. In a 2010 interview at a technology conference, Jobs verbalized Apple's do-more-with-less mentality. "Apple is a company that doesn't have the most resources," he said, referring to Apple's response to a technical debate raging at the time. "And the way we've succeeded is by choosing which horses to ride very

WHAT HAPPENS AT 1 INFINITE LOOP

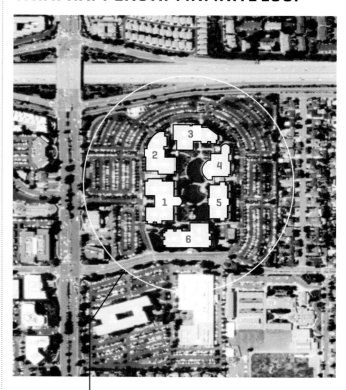

Apple's headquarters in Cupertino, Calif., consist of six buildings on its main campus. Its iTunes business operates out of multiple buildings nearby.

Building 1
Executive team

Building 2
Software engineering

Building 3
Marketing and communications

Building 4
Town Hall auditorium and cafeteria

Building 5
Sales

Building 6
Hardware engineering

carefully." On the face of it, the statement is absurd. Times certainly once were tough at Apple, breeding an underdog culture. Today, with $66 billion in the bank, nothing could be further from the truth, yet Apple continues to behave like a scrappy upstart. "We've always fought for resources," says a former executive. "Steve and Tim in general want to be sure you need what you're asking for."

Apple insiders say the notion of scarce resources has less to do with money than it does with finding enough people to perform critical tasks. Once Apple moves, though, it spends

DIGITAL GLOBE

whatever it takes. It contracted the London Symphony Orchestra to record trailer soundtracks for its latest iMovie software. Years ago it sent a camera crew to Hawaii to film a wedding for a demo video; then, to get a different take, it staged fake nuptials in a San Francisco church, with Apple employees playing both guests and the betrothed.

Learning to work at Apple takes time. To echo its own famous ad campaign, Apple thinks differently about business. Often as not it simply ignores traditional notions of business opportunities. An executive who has worked at Apple and Microsoft describes the differences this way: "Microsoft tries to find pockets of unrealized revenue and then figures out what to make. Apple is just the opposite: It thinks of great products, then sells them. Prototypes and demos always come before spreadsheets."

Specialization is the norm at Apple, and as a result, Apple employees aren't exposed to functions outside their area of expertise. Jennifer Bailey, the executive who runs Apple's online store, for example, has no authority over the photographs on the site. Photographic images are handled companywide by Apple's graphic arts department. Apple's powerful retail chief, Ron Johnson, doesn't control the inventory in his stores. Tim Cook, whose background is in supply-chain management, handles inventory across the company. (Johnson has plenty left to do, including site selection, in-store service, and store layout.)

Jobs sees such specialization as a process of having best-in-class employees in every role, and he has no patience for building managers for the sake of managing. "Steve would say the general manager structure is bullshit," says Mike Janes, the former Apple executive. "It creates fiefdoms." Instead, rising stars are invited to attend executive team meetings as guests to expose them to the decision-making process. It is the polar opposite of the General Electric-like notion of creating well-rounded executives.

Such rigidity—coupled with the threat of being called on the carpet by Jobs—would seem to make Apple an impossibly difficult workplace, yet recruiters say turnover at Apple is exceedingly low. "It is a happy place in that it has true believers," says a headhunter who has worked extensively with Apple to hire engineers. "People join and stay because they believe in the mission of the company, even if they aren't personally happy." Many of Apple's rank-and-file technical employees have dreamed of working at Apple since they got their first Macs as children. "At Apple you work on Apple products. If you're a diehard Apple geek, it's magical," says Andrew Borovsky, the former designer. "But it's also a really tough place to work." In short, it is an environment that shuns coddling. "Apple's attitude is, 'You have the privilege of working for the company that's making the fucking coolest products in the world,'" says one former product management executive. "'Shut up and do your job, and you might get to stay.'"

FOR YEARS STEVE JOBS was uninterested in the human resources department at Apple. Then, three years ago, just before his second medical leave, he hired Joel Podolny, dean of the Yale School of Management, to head something called Apple University. Podolny had been a widely quoted management guru. Yet when he joined Apple, typically, he vanished from sight. No one even seemed to notice when he was named vice president of human resources a couple of years later.

It turns out that Podolny has been busy working on a project that speaks directly to the delicate topic of life at Apple after Jobs. At Jobs' instruction, Podolny hired a team of business professors, including the renowned Harvard veteran and Andy Grove biographer Richard Tedlow. This band of eggheads is writing a series of internal case studies about significant decisions in Apple's recent history. It's exactly the sort of thing the major business schools do, except Apple's case studies are for an Apple-only audience. Top executives, including Tim Cook and Ron Johnson, teach the cases, which have covered subjects including the decision to consolidate iPhone manufacturing around a single factory in China and the establishment of Apple's stores. The goal is to expose the next layer of management to the executive team's thought process.

All this raises the question of whether Jobs has adequately prepared Apple for the day he isn't around anymore. It's an impossible question to answer. According to one person who knows Jobs, he acknowledges his dictatorial powers but insists he's not the only one who can wield them. "Single-cell organisms aren't interesting," he told this person. "Apple is a complex, multicellular organism."

Those who believe Apple can't survive Jobs' departure—and there are many—would call this wishful thinking. Apple may be a multicellular organism, but its life source is Jobs. For now this is all in the realm of opinion. Jobs himself believes he has set Apple on a course to survive in his absence. He has created a culture that, while not particularly jolly, has internalized his ways. Jobs even is ensuring that his teachings are being collected, curated, and preserved so that future generations of Apple's leaders can consult and interpret them. It's about all a savior could possibly ask for.

Reporting by Doris Burke

The Legacy of Steve Jobs

Chapter One

Dan Saelinger

Fortune
March 17,
2008

WHAT MAKES APPLE GOLDEN: AN EXCLUSIVE INTERVIEW WITH STEVE JOBS

THE CREATOR OF THE iPOD AND iPHONE SETS A DAZZLING NEW STANDARD FOR INNOVATION AND MASS APPEAL, DRIVEN BY AN OBSESSIVE CEO WHO WANTS HIS PRODUCTS TO BE PRACTICALLY PERFECT IN EVERY WAY.

BY BETSY MORRIS

Fortune senior editor Betsy Morris spoke with Jobs in February 2008 in Kona, Hawaii, where he was vacationing with his family, about the keys to Apple's success, obstacles along the way, and the prospect of Apple without Steve Jobs.

On the birth of the iPhone: We all had cellphones. They were so awful to use. The software was terrible. The hardware wasn't very good. We talked to our friends, and they all hated their cellphones too. And we saw that these things really could become much more powerful. It's a huge market. I mean, a billion phones get shipped every year, and that's almost an order of magnitude greater than the number of music players. It's four times the number of PCs that ship every year.

It was a great challenge: Let's make a great phone that we fall in love with. Nobody had ever thought about putting operating systems as sophisticated as OS X inside a phone, so that was a real question. We had a big debate inside the company whether we could do that or not. And that was one where I had to adjudicate it and just say, "We're going to do it. Let's try." The smartest software guys were saying they can do it, so let's give them a shot. And they did.

On Apple's connection with the consumer: It's not about pop culture, and it's not about fooling people, and it's not about convincing people that they want something they don't. We figure out what we want. And I think we're pretty good at having the right discipline to think through whether a lot of other people are going to want it too. That's what we get paid to do.

On choosing strategy: We do no market research. We just want to make great products. When we created the iTunes Music Store, we did that because we thought it would be great to be able to buy music electronically, not because we had plans to redefine the music industry. I mean, it just seemed like writing on the wall that eventually all music would be distributed electronically. Why have all this [cost] when you can just send electrons around easily?

On Apple's focus: People think focus means saying yes to the thing you've got to focus on. But that's not what it means at all. It means saying no to the 100 other good ideas that there are. You have to pick carefully. I'm actually as proud of many of the things we haven't done as the things we have done. The clearest example was when we were pressured for years to do a PDA, and I realized one day that 90% of the people who use a PDA only take information out of it on the road. They don't put information into it. Pretty soon cellphones are going to do that, so the PDA market's going

to get reduced to a fraction of its current size. So we decided not to get into it. If we had gotten into it, we wouldn't have had the resources to do the iPod.

On what drives Apple employees: We don't get a chance to do that many things, and every one should be really excellent. Because this is our life. Life is brief, and then you die, you know? So this is what we've chosen to do with our life. We could be sitting in a monastery somewhere in Japan. We could be out sailing. Some of the [executive team] could be playing golf. They could be running other companies. And we've all chosen to do this with our lives. So it'd better be damn good.

On why people want to work at Apple: The reason is because you can't do what you can do at Apple anywhere else. The engineering is long gone in PC companies. In the consumer electronics companies, they don't understand the software parts of it. And so you really can't make the products that you can make at Apple anywhere else right now. Apple's the only company that has everything under one roof. There's no other company that could make a MacBook Air, and the reason is that not only do we control the hardware, but we control the operating system. And it is the intimate interaction between the operating system and the hardware that allows us to do that. There is no intimate interaction between Windows and a Dell notebook.

On whether Apple could live without him: We've got really capable people at Apple. I made Tim [Cook] COO and gave him the Mac division, and he's done brilliantly. I mean, some people say, "Oh, God, if [Jobs] got run over by a bus, Apple would be in trouble." And, you know, I think it wouldn't be a party, but the board would have some good choices about who to pick as CEO. My job is to make the whole executive team good enough to be successors, so that's what I try to do.

On his demanding reputation: My job is to not be easy on people. My job is to take these great people we have and to push them and make them even better. How? Just by coming up with more aggressive visions of how it could be.

On dealing with roadblocks: There always seems to come a moment where it's just not working. Take the iPhone. We had a different enclosure design for this iPhone until way too close to the introduction to ever change it. And I came in one Monday morning, and I said, "I just don't love this. I can't convince myself to fall in love with this. And this is the most important product we've ever done." And we pushed the reset button. We went through all the zillions of models we'd made and ideas we'd had. And we ended up creating what you see here as the iPhone, which is dramatically better. It was hell because we had to go to the team and say, "All this work you've [done] for the last year, we're going to have to throw it away and start over, and we're going to have to work twice as hard now because we don't have enough time." And you know what everybody said? "Sign us up." That happens more than you'd think, because this is not just engineering and science. There is art too. Sometimes when you're in the middle of one of these crises, you're not sure you're going to make it to the other end. But we've always made it, and so we have a certain degree of confidence, although sometimes you wonder.

On his management style: We've got 25,000 people at Apple. About 10,000 of them are in the stores. And my job is to work with sort of the top 100 people—that's what I do. That doesn't mean they're all vice presidents. Some of them are just key individual contributors. So when a good idea comes, part of my job is to move it around, just see what different people think, get people talking about it, argue with people about it, get ideas moving among that group of 100 people.

On his marathon Monday meetings: When you hire really good people, you have to give them a piece of the business and let them run with it. That doesn't mean I don't get to kibitz a lot. But the reason you're hiring them is because you're going to give them the reins. I want [them] making as good or better decisions than I would. So the way to do that is to have them know everything, not just in their part of the business but in every part of the business. So what we do every Monday is we review the whole business. We look at what we sold the week before. We look at every product under development—products we're having trouble with, products where the demand is larger than we can meet. All the stuff in development, we review.

On finding talent: When I hire somebody really senior, competence is the ante. They have to be really smart. But the real issue for me is, Are they going to fall in love with Apple? Because if they fall in love with Apple, everything else will take care of itself. They'll want to do what's best for Apple, not what's best for them, what's best for Steve, or anybody else.

Recruiting is hard. It's finding the needles in the haystack. I've participated in the hiring of maybe 5,000-plus people in my life. I take it very seriously. You can't know enough in a one-hour interview. So in the end, it's ultimately based on your gut. How do I feel about this person? What are they like when they're challenged? Why are they here? I ask everybody that: "Why are you here?" The answers themselves are not what you're looking for. It's the meta-data.

On the iPod tipping point: It was difficult for a while because for various reasons the Mac had not been accepted by a lot of people, who went with Windows. And we were just working really hard, and our market share wasn't going up. It makes you wonder sometimes whether you're wrong. Maybe our stuff isn't better, although we thought it was. Or maybe people don't care, which is even more depressing.

It turns out with the iPod we got out from that operating-system glass ceiling. It was great because [it showed that] Apple innovation, Apple engineering, Apple design did matter. The iPod captured 70% market share. I cannot tell you how important that was to Apple after so many years of laboring and seeing a 4% to 5% market share on the Mac. It was a great shot in the arm for everybody.

On catching tech's next wave: Things happen fairly slowly, you know. They do. These waves of technology, you can see them way before they happen, and you just have to choose wisely which ones you're going to surf. If you choose unwisely, then you can waste a lot of energy, but if you choose wisely, it actually unfolds fairly slowly. It takes years. One of our biggest insights [years ago] was that we didn't want to get into any business where we didn't own or control the primary technology, because you'll get your head handed to you. We realized that for almost all future consumer electronics, the primary technology was going to be software. And we were pretty good at software. We could do the operating system software. We could write applications like iTunes on the Mac or even PC. We could write the software in the device, like you might put in an iPod or an iPhone. And we could write the back-end software that runs on a cloud, like iTunes. So we could write all these different kinds of software and tweed it all together and make it work seamlessly. And you ask yourself, What other companies can do that? It's a pretty short list.

On managing through the economic downturn: We've had one of these before, when the dot-com bubble burst. What I told our company was that we were just going to invest our way through the downturn, that we weren't going to lay off people, that we'd taken a tremendous amount of effort to get them into Apple in the first place—the last thing we were going to do is lay them off. And we were going to keep funding. In fact we were going to up our R&D budget so that we would be ahead of our competitors when the downturn was over. And that's exactly what we did. And it worked. And that's exactly what we'll do this time.

Chapter Two

THE EARLY YEARS

Jobs and Steve Wozniak launched the company in Jobs' parents' garage in 1976. By the early 1980s, Jobs had built Apple into an industry powerhouse with the Apple II and the Mac. Those days were far from easy, however. These stories chronicled how a scrappy upstart held its own against a formidable IBM and its popular PC. Then came slowing sales and bitter infighting between Jobs and John Sculley, the PepsiCo executive brought in to put Apple back on course. Jobs tried to oust Sculley, but he failed and was forced out of the company. During his exile, Jobs founded Next Computer; the operating system developed there ended up driving today's Macs. He also helped build a small animation company named Pixar, which eventually launched blockbusters such as *Toy Story* and *Finding Nemo* and made Jobs a billionaire.

JOBS AT WORK IN 1984. **PHOTOGRAPH BY NORMAN SEEFF**

APPLE'S TO STAY IN THE BIG TIME

BY PETER NULTY

Apple
vs.
IBM sales

According to International Data Corp., a market research firm, Apple's growth, though still strong, slackened significantly after IBM arrived. Hardest hit is the Apple III business computer.

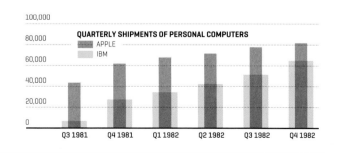

QUARTERLY SHIPMENTS OF PERSONAL COMPUTERS
APPLE
IBM

CONTOUR BY GETTY

JOBS AT APPLE HEADQUARTERS

"**I GET MY JOLLIES BUILDING GOOD COMPUTERS,**" says Steven P. Jobs, 27, chairman of Apple Computer. Critics of Apple's product line might assume Jobs hasn't had a good belly laugh in some time. Apple's first and, so far, only big winner is the Apple II, six years old and showing signs of age. But during the past three years Apple has been working on a new computer called Lisa. Jobs is betting that Lisa—though five times the price of the Apple II and aimed at a different market—will keep him jolly by keeping his company in the forefront of a rapidly changing industry.

In a series of interviews before Lisa's introduction this week, Apple detailed for *Fortune* the technical and marketing strategies that shaped the new product. These were designed to capitalize on the company's acknowledged strengths. No company has done more than Apple to dispel the notion that computers are inscrutable beasts. Indeed, demystifying the machine has been Apple's greatest strength.

THE COMPANY TOOK OFF IN 1977 with the Apple II, one of the first personal computers that wasn't a hobbyist's kit. The machine fit easily on a desktop, cost less than $3,000, and sported the industry's least intimidating logo, a rainbow-colored apple with one big bite missing. Apple encouraged thousands of independent programmers to invent applications for the Apple II, and the result is a library of 16,000 software programs. These range from such games as Snack Attack to budget analysis programs like VisiCalc and farm-management programs like Swine Ration Formulation, which tells farmers how much to feed their pigs. At its core, Apple II isn't easier to use than other small computers, but straightforward engineering, good design, clever marketing, and all those programs have so far enticed over 700,000 buyers.

Lisa draws heavily on Apple's talent for disarming computer-phobes. The new machine, which bears a hefty $10,000 price tag and is aimed at the office market, is set apart from other computers by ease of operation. Lisa is, pardon the computer jargon, exceedingly user-friendly, if not outright seductive. She turns the tedious chore of drafting office reports into something close to playing a video game.

Unveiled on Jan. 19, with first shipments sometime in the spring, Lisa comes none too soon for Apple, although sales in 1982 reached $583 million (up 74% from 1981), and net earnings were $61 million, or $1.06 per share, up 51%. Apple went public late in 1980, selling shares for $22 each.

JOBS AT HIS CUPERTINO HOME

Since then, the stock has gone as high as $35 and as low as $10. Now it's selling for about $30.

Those numbers mask some disconcerting facts. The Apple II is a six-year-old machine competing in a market where technology improves almost daily. Moreover, Apple has yet to prove it is capable of repeating its success. In 1981 the firm tried expanding the product line with the Apple III, a more powerful version of the Apple II aimed at offices. But the Apple III was so full of worms that the first 14,000 were recalled, and the machine was eventually re-engineered. The second version of the Apple III is not selling very well. Ulric Weil, a security analyst at Morgan Stanley, estimates Apple III is selling between 3,000 and 3,500 a month. Apple II sales are now close to 30,000 a month.

During the Apple III debacle, the company lost time, face, and a good piece of the office market to the phenomenally successful IBM Personal Computer. The PC, as IBM's machine is called, owes its success mainly to IBM's reputation and a skillful introduction. Big Blue's logo on the front inspires customer confidence that no other company can match. The PC is now selling at the rate of about 20,000 per month.

DIANA WALKER—SJ/CONTOUR BY GETTY

Apple watchers have been increasingly wondering whether the invention and success of the Apple II owed more to luck than to savvy. The company's sales force has been meeting resistance in stores. Says one marketing manager: "Apple III has a stigma attached to it. And Apple II? How can we expect our salesmen to sell the same dingdong product in this market for five years running?" The firm was able to keep Apple II sales up during the past six months principally by offering package deals that effectively cut the list price by about 25%.

Although Lisa is the first really easy-to-use personal computer, she is not much for looks—a chunky box with an overhanging brow reminiscent of the primitive visage of an ape. But that impression is totally misleading. Inside the box, Lisa contains a microprocessor that can manipulate data in many cases four times faster than the Apple II or III and twice as quickly as the IBM PC. In addition, Lisa has the memory of an elephant. The processor's main memory alone can hold one million bytes of data, or roughly 160,000 words. Attached to the central processing unit are two floppy-disk drives, which Apple designed for Lisa, and one hard-disk drive. Total external memory: 6.7 million bytes.

LISA'S MOST DISTINGUISHING FEATURE, though, is the massive programming Apple engineers have stored in her memory. To operate even the simplest personal computers today, a user must learn a myriad of arcane commands and procedures. The industry calls this computer literacy. Apple engineers have taught Lisa to be people-literate.

Lisa takes orders primarily from a mouse, not a keyboard. The mouse is a cigarette-pack-size plastic box with a button on top and a cable connected to the computer. When the mouse is moved on the surface of a desk, an arrow moves on Lisa's TV-like monitor screen. This permits the user to juggle words or statistics around in much the same way that a child uses a joystick to manipulate spaceships in a video game. Lisa also has a standard keyboard, but the operator has to use it only to type in text or statistics.

This deceptively simple system should save computer neophytes days, or even weeks, in learning to use the machine. For example, it takes about 20 hours of practice to become handy with a business budget, or "spreadsheet," program like VisiCalc on an Apple II. The rankest amateur will need only an hour or so to operate a similar program on Lisa.

The ease of use is also increased because the commands are the same for all Lisa programs. With other personal computers, an executive who has spent several days mastering a word-processing program usually must then spend a similar amount of time learning spreadsheet accounting or any other programs. Initially, Lisa will include six basic functions: word processing, graphics, spreadsheet analysis, database management, project scheduling, and drawing. By Apple's estimates, a novice should be able to learn all six in a day. It might take a month to master those skills on other computers.

Another of Lisa's features is the ability to swap information between programs. Budget estimates, for example, can be transferred to the graph program and turned into a bar or pie chart. Then both the statistics and the chart can be incorporated into a memo being drafted with the word-processing program. The sharing of commands and the flow of information from one program to another, known as integration, is a major goal of the software industry in the 1980s. Some integrated programs like C-MBA and 1-2-3, much less ambitious than Lisa's, have already been introduced.

TEACHING LISA HER TRICKS was a major undertaking. The programs, which are permanently stored in Lisa's memory, contain a staggering 2 million bytes of information. The internal Apple II programming, by comparison, has only 16,000 bytes, and the Apple III contains 200,000. Three years in the making, Lisa's software alone devoured $20 million and 200 man-years of labor. John D. Couch, 35, the Lisa manager, estimates the total startup cost of Lisa will reach $50 million. "If we had known how big Lisa would get," says Couch, "I'm not sure we would have begun at all."

The whole project started with the notion of user-friendliness. When the Apple II began selling briskly in 1977 and 1978, the company was surprised to find that a large number of the machines were going into offices. At that point Apple faced a fundamental decision on market strategy. Should it go after the home computer market or the business market? Apple decided to go to the office, where profit margins are higher and its new product's advanced technology would show off better. Says Jobs: "I figured that we could sell five or 10 times as many computers in the office if they were easy to use."

Jobs' first task was to lasso talent, and John Couch was his initial recruit. The two met in 1978 when Couch, then 30, was a rising young manager at Hewlett-Packard. They agreed that software would be the key to success in the computer field and that good software had to be easy to use.

Couch scuttled his career at Hewlett-Packard, taking a cut in salary from $55,000 to $40,000 and reducing his management responsibility from 141 people to none. Both cuts, as it turned out, were temporary.

When the idea of an easy-to-use computer got rolling, Jobs and Couch had no trouble convincing others of its dazzling promise. The project at present employs 140 engineers and programmers, mostly in their 20s. Eighteen programmers followed Couch from Hewlett-Packard. Lisa's chief engineer, Wayne Rosing, 36, came from Digital Equipment Corp. One day in 1980, Rosing was on a quick trip to California when he stopped in to see Couch on the recommendation of a friend. Within minutes he knew he wanted to work for Apple. By the next day he had a deal with Couch and phoned Digital to resign. Four colleagues from Digital joined him at Apple. Lawrence G. Tesler, 37, who was the software manager for Lisa, was formerly a computer researcher for Xerox. In December 1979 he was demonstrating some techniques in computer friendliness Xerox had developed to a troupe of Apple engineers and marketing executives led by Jobs and Couch. "I was expecting a bunch of hobbyists," Tesler recalls, "and was impressed to find people sophisticated in computer science." Tesler decided on the spot to join Apple.

That day of briefings at Xerox was the turning point in Lisa's development. Although Jobs and Couch had been brainstorming about the project, occasionally while sipping brandy in the hot tub at Couch's house in Los Gatos, and company engineers had been busy building prototypes of a new machine, the critical software remained only a vague concept. The Xerox researchers demonstrated a programming language called Smalltalk that worked with a mouse. Suddenly the possibilities became apparent.

Xerox has since incorporated some features of Smalltalk into a product called Star. While a technological marvel, Star has not sold well since its introduction in April 1981. Each Star computer costs $16,600 and won't work well unless hooked up to a large disk drive costing $55,000 or more. According to industry rumors, Xerox is working on a smaller, less expensive version of Star. E. David Crockett, senior vice president of Dataquest, a market research firm in Cupertino, California, says Xerox is selling about 100 to 200 Stars per month. "It's a product looking for a home," he says. In one sense, it has found a home at Apple.

The Apple group resolved to create on Lisa's screen the look and procedures of an everyday office. To do this, they have used pictures to represent certain procedures—a wastebasket for the disposal of information, a clipboard for temporary storage, a folder for filing data. But they soon discovered that even the simplest improvement demanded much more software. The mouse on Xerox's Star, for example, has two different command buttons. It took the Apple team six months to reduce their mouse's buttons from two to one.

Wayne Rosing recalls that one of the issues they had to resolve was how to show the wastebasket on the screen. When a trash can is drawn the size of a thumbnail, it has almost no distinguishing characteristics. So to make the picture understandable, Apple's programmers playfully added a few flies buzzing around the top. That was too palsy-walsy for Rosing, who feared Lisa would become the butt of jokes. Eventually the flies were replaced by a lid, slightly askew. The image is less vivid, but clear.

While Apple was trying to keep Lisa under wraps, word of the project leaked out about 18 months ago. When the machine did not appear on the market as soon as expected, speculation grew that Lisa was being delayed to avert the kind of recall disaster that befell the Apple III. Jobs admits that the Apple III experience slowed Lisa down a bit. But, he says, "Lisa was just bigger than we anticipated. Scheduling is an art. Most of Lisa's software was created from scratch, and that's very hard to predict."

THE GREATEST MYSTERY of all in the Lisa development was how to integrate the different computer applications, such as word-processing, statistical, and graphics programs, so that the user could easily swap material. Tesler says he estimated in 1980 it would take anywhere from two months to two years to accomplish that. Years was closer to the mark. By last summer, however, the programs were beginning to come together. One July afternoon, Tesler recalls, the programmers succeeded in getting all six application programs on the screen at the same time. Lisa was expertly pulling the budget report, for instance, out of the middle of the pile of documents and then putting it in full view on top.

To celebrate their achievement, the programmers broke out bottles of Stanford, a California champagne (price: $4.29 per bottle). Soon feeling giddy, some people decided to work on the next project: moving the data from within one program to another. The schedule allotted two weeks for this development, but with their champagne-induced confidence, the programmers had it working within hours. So they had a second champagne party that night—this time uncorking Korbel, which is twice as expensive as Stanford. "Since then, there have been a lot of parties," says Tesler.

"But we really knew we had done well when the marketing department started paying for the bubbly."

If Lisa sells well, the marketing department will deserve a party in return. Many industry watchers agree with Dataquest's David Crockett, who says, "Apple is taking on a new market and a new product at the same time. Typically, that means a slow start."

Apple expects more than a third of Lisa's sales in the first year will be to the 2,300 U.S. companies with over $120 million in annual revenue. Big corporations, however, will be relatively new territory for Apple, which has marketed its other machines to small firms and hobbyists, mainly through a network of 1,300 independent retailers. The company has organized a sales staff of 100 so-called national account representatives who will work with about 100 of the independent retailers to tackle the new market. Sales may be difficult. Apple will be going directly up against IBM. Distribution thus is expected to be a serious problem for Apple.

Even before Lisa was introduced, Apple already faced competition. VisiCorp, the publishers of the best-selling VisiCalc program, announced that this summer it will begin selling a product called VisiOn, a system of integrated software that works with a mouse. VisiCorp claims that it will provide many of Lisa's features at a lower cost for IBM and Digital personal computers. But a demonstration model of VisiOn, which the company has been showing since November, appears more limited than Lisa. Terry L. Opdendyk, VisiCorp's president, promises the final product will be more powerful. However, no one can be certain about the cost or delivery date of VisiOn. Computer projects are well known for being both late and over budget.

PERHAPS THE GREATEST QUESTION facing Lisa is cost. Will companies pay the $10,000 price? Though much cheaper than Xerox's Star, that is more than twice the price of the normally equipped IBM PC. Much will depend on Apple's still undetermined volume-discount policy. Says Jonathan Seybold, an editor of the *Seybold Report on Office Automation*, which tested the machine for two weeks: "Lisa is clearly a milestone product. After Lisa the professional computing world will never be the same again. But the price is at the very high end of the acceptable range. I think that the right price for Lisa would have been $7,500."

Lisa is not the only new Apple in Jobs' basket. The company has also just unveiled an updated version of the Apple II, the IIE. And later this year Apple will introduce a less powerful, less expensive version of Lisa, the Macintosh. Jobs himself has directed that project.

Apple's new products will leave the firm with a slightly confused and overlapping line of old and new personal computers. The old-generation Apple IIE has a basic list price of $1,395, while that of the Apple III is $2,995. The new-generation Lisa will be $10,000, but the Macintosh may be as little as $2,000. Even though the Macintosh may be delayed and end up costing much more, rumors about it could hurt Lisa's sales. And in the end, the Macintosh may be Apple's real winner.

One of the most difficult stages in the development of a young, entrepreneurial firm like Apple comes when it tries to repeat its initial success with a new product. Companies in fields as diverse as cars and calculators have stumbled and lost the market they once dominated. Lisa and Macintosh will determine whether Apple joins those failures or remains among the leaders of the computer industry.

LISA'S MOUSE (FOREGROUND) TAKES A LOT OF THE COMPLEXITY OUT OF OPERATING THE COMPUTER. THE KEYBOARD IS USED FOR ENTERING TEXT AND NUMBERS INTO THE MACHINE. THE MOUSE GIVES THE COMMANDS.

CHARLES O'REAR

A HISTORY OF APPLE

Since Apple's inception in 1976, Steve Jobs has been on a roller-coaster ride that ultimately paid off for the company's shareholders. If you had invested $100 in Apple stock at the beginning of 1983, it would now equal $10,211. The same amount invested in the S&P 500-stock index would be worth only $805, as the chart below shows.

2005

Jobs undergoes cancer surgery, discloses both cancer and "cure" the next day.

2005

iPod Nano is released. Huge hit.

1995

Pixar releases *Toy Story*, the first full-length computer-animated film, to rave reviews.

Pixar goes public one week later; Jobs' 80% stake is worth $585 million.

1996

Apple announces acquisition of Next for $430 million, posts $816 million loss for the year.

1997

Jobs becomes interim CEO of Apple, replaces board, launches "Think different" campaign.

1998

Apple returns to profitability. The iMac debuts, becomes the fastest-selling Macintosh ever.

2000

Jobs becomes permanent CEO of Apple. Board gives Jobs a Gulfstream V jet and 40 million options.

2001

Big year for introductions: first Apple Stores, the iPod, iTunes, and the OS X operating system.

1976

Apple Computer is founded. Apple I is introduced.

1979

Jobs and a team of engineers visit Xerox PARC, where they see a demo of mouse and graphical user interface.

1980

Apple goes public in biggest IPO since Ford Motor in 1956. Jobs' 15% stake is worth more than $200 million.

1983

The Apple Lisa is released, inspired by Xerox's user interface.

1984

The Macintosh is introduced. The "1984" commercial airs during the Super Bowl.

1985

Jobs is ousted from Apple. Launches Next, pays Paul Rand $100,000 to design logo.

1986

Jobs buys Pixar from George Lucas for $10 million.

1988

The Next Cube is released. Price: $6,500.

1984 NORMAN SEEFF

$1,000

VALUE OF $100 INVESTED IN AAPL VS. S&P 500 INDEX

$100

| 1976 | 1977 | 1978 | 1979 | 1980 | 1981 | 1982 | 1983 | 1984 | 1985 | 1986 | 1987 | 1988 | 1989 | 1990 | 1991 | 1992 |

2006

Pixar is sold to Disney, making Jobs its largest shareholder, with a stake now worth $4.6 billion.

2007

Jobs reveals the highly anticipated iPhone, which becomes a sensation; he also shows an Apple TV device for iTunes content, which flops.

2007

Tenth anniversary of Jobs' return to Apple.

2008

Jobs unveils the world's thinnest notebook, the MacBook Air.

Jobs, noticeably skinnier, flashes slide reading, "Reports of my death are greatly exaggerated" at an Apple event.

2009

Jobs announces leave of absence; names Tim Cook to run day-to-day operations.

Jobs undergoes liver transplant surgery in Memphis.

2009

Jobs, in his first public appearance since transplant, hosts an Apple music event.

2010

Launch of the iPad.

2011

Launch of iCloud.

Jobs resignation: Aug. 24.

$10,000

$9,000

$8,000

2003

Former Vice President Al Gore joins Apple's board.

iTunes Music Store opens and rocks the music industry with 99¢ pricing for songs.

The Power Mac G5 becomes the world's fastest personal computer. Jobs swaps underwater options for restricted shares.

Jobs is diagnosed with pancreatic cancer; board decides not to disclose it.

$7,000

$6,000

$5,000

$4,000

$3,000

APPLE STOCK RETURNS

$2,000

S&P 500 INDEX RETURNS

'94 1995 1996 1997 1998 1999 2000 2001 2002 2003 2004 2005 2006 2007 2008 2009 2010 2011

PLATIAU—REUTERS; BLOOMBERG/GETTY; 2011: JUSTIN SULLIVAN—GETTY

CHART NOTE: VALUES NOT ADJUSTED FOR DISTRIBUTIONS.

 The Legacy of Steve Jobs

 Chapter Two

 Ed Kashi

 Fortune
August 5,
1985

CHAIRMAN STEVE
JOBS [LEFT] WITH
CHIEF EXECUTIVE JOHN
SCULLEY IN OCTOBER
1984 IN HAWAII

CORBIS

BEHIND THE FALL OF STEVE JOBS

THE BOARD PRESSED CEO JOHN SCULLEY TO SEIZE THE REINS OF APPLE. WHEN HE DID, JOBS TRIED TO OUST HIM. NOW COMES THE HARD PART FOR THE SHAKEN COMPANY.

BY BRO UTTAL

IGH ON THE LIST of Apple Computer's talents is "event marketing"—turning corporate announcements into extravaganzas that reap lavish press coverage. Lately, though, the press has been trumpeting events that the Cupertino, Calif., company would prefer not to publicize at all. From the end of May to the middle of June, Apple reorganized in a rush, fired 20% of its workforce, announced that it would record its first-ever quarterly loss, saw its stock hit a three-year low of $4.25 a share, and stripped Steven P. Jobs, Apple's 30-year-old co-founder and chairman, of all operating authority. John Sculley, 46, president and chief executive, ruefully remarked that Apple's moves were attracting as much attention as an episode of *Dynasty*.

Jobs' fate has aroused intense speculation. Not just another brash young entrepreneur, he is the Johnny Appleseed of personal computing, the leading broadcaster of "technology for the people." Until June, Jobs led the development and marketing of the Macintosh computer, an easy-to-use, technologically advanced machine on which Apple has staked its future. Many insiders are shocked by his removal; they fear Apple has lost the spirit and vision that made it into a business phenomenon. Says one: "They've cut the heart out of Apple and substituted an artificial one. We'll just have to see how long it pumps."

No players in the drama have explained publicly why Jobs came to grief. But several of them, promised anonymity, have revealed the essential details to *Fortune*. Though Jobs, a celebrated visionary, and Sculley, a driven corporate professional, are radically different personalities, they formed a strong bond. Sculley seems to retain an unusual affection for Jobs even today. "I decided to change my life and come to Apple," he says, "because of my admiration for Steve and what he had done. Our reorganization was all the more painful because we are such close friends."

What emerges from Apple sources is a tale of adversity— a general slump in the personal computer business and disappointing sales at the Mac division—driving a wedge between Sculley and Jobs. Apple's board of directors, with strong-minded outsiders such as Arthur Rock, the San Francisco venture capitalist, played an important part in Jobs' downfall. On several occasions, beginning last December, the board goaded Sculley to assert his authority over the company. Even then, Sculley put off acting, partly from innate caution about radical organizational change and partly out of concern for Jobs' feelings. But Sculley was forced to

reorganize, thus neutralizing Jobs, when he learned that the chairman was plotting to depose him.

Viewed dispassionately, Apple's reorganization is a further step in an overhaul Sculley has been working on slowly since May 1983, when Jobs wooed him away from the presidency of Pepsi-Cola USA, the beverage subsidiary of PepsiCo. From the beginning, Sculley says, his mission was to teach Apple marketing and improve its response to retailers and customers. That meant merging the company's nine highly decentralized divisions, most of which had broad responsibility for a product line, into an organization structured according to such business functions as engineering, manufacturing, and marketing. One marketing group, for example, would handle advertising and promotion for all Apple products.

Transforming Apple was a tougher task than Sculley first imagined. Under Jobs the company had acquired a near-maniacal focus on products: The chairman electrified Apple's corps with talk of "insanely great" new computers, and he made stars of product designers. By the beginning of 1984, though, Sculley had managed to consolidate Apple's divisions into just three: a sales division for all products, a division for the Apple II family of products, and one with the forthcoming Macintosh as its centerpiece and Jobs as its general manager.

The organization appeared to work at first. Under Delbert W. Yocam, 41, a sober, buttoned-up Apple veteran who had risen through manufacturing, the Apple II division turned in a record performance. In calendar 1984 it sold an estimated 800,000 Apple IIe's and portable IIc's, ringing up revenues of nearly $1 billion. William V. Campbell, 44, an aggressive marketer and former football coach whom Sculley had hired away from Eastman Kodak, managed in less than two months to hire and train 360 people for Apple's field force selling to dealers. Jobs' division, having launched the Macintosh in January, sold some 250,000 Macs by year-end, fewer than its goal but more than the legendary IBM

ED KASHI—CORBIS

PC had achieved in its first year. The Mac division pulled in revenues of some $500 million, though the costs of introduction ate into profits.

Hairline cracks in the Jobs-Sculley partnership showed up around October, as friction between the two product groups heated up. The Mac division, whose managers Apple had publicized as superstars, considered itself the company's elite. That spirit had helped it develop the technologically sophisticated Macintosh on a crash schedule, but it irritated Yocam's group. The Apple II division was producing more of the company's sales and most of the profits, yet the Mac division seemed to get all the perks. For a time these included free fruit juice and a masseur on call.

According to several insiders, Jobs, a devout believer that new technology should supersede the old, couldn't abide the success of the venerable Apple II. Nor did he hide his feelings. He once addressed the Apple II marketing staff as members of the "dull and boring product division." As chairman and largest stockholder, with an 11.3% block, Jobs was a disproportionately powerful general manager. And he had disproportionate enthusiasm for the Mac staff. Says one of them: "He was so protective of us that whenever we complained about somebody outside the division, it was like unleashing a Doberman. Steve would get on the telephone and chew the guy out so fast your head would spin."

An executive who has left the Apple II division recalls seeing things from a different perspective: "We used to say that the Mac people had God on their team." In February, Steve Wozniak, the company's other co-founder, designer of the original Apple computer and an engineer in Yocam's group, left in a huff.

APPLE MIGHT HAVE ENDURED these rivalries without a major upheaval had it not been for mounting business pressures. The company's stunning Christmas quarter, which lends a false sheen to reported results for the four quarters through March 1985, was followed by a worrisome winter and spring. For the first time ever, Apple had no back orders left over from Christmas; dealers were wallowing in inventory. Apple earned a record $46 million on sales of $698 million in the Christmas quarter, largely on the strength of the Apple II. But it cleared only $10 million on sales of $435 million for the three months that ended March 29. That was hardly more than the company's profits of $9.1 million on far smaller sales of $300 million for the comparable quarter of 1984.

Jobs' Macintosh division had planned on selling 150,000 Macs over the Christmas season but fell short by 50,000

or so. Mac sales declined to an average of only 19,000 units a month in the first quarter of 1985, then fell further. Apple's stepped-up effort to sell the machine to businesses was making no headway. Some Apple executives blamed Michael Murray, 30, then director of Mac marketing. Research showed that the messages Murray had been trying to send the market weren't getting through. Recalls a former Mac staffer: "Mac was being perceived as a cutesy avocado machine for yuppies and their kids, not as an office machine or as the technology leader that it is." But product development was also in disarray. Jobs and his director of engineering, Robert L. Belleville, a brilliant designer, were missing schedules for crucial parts of the Mac system. They were months behind, for example, with a large disk drive that would help Mac run sophisticated software programs for business and make it easier for users to share information.

As Mac sales kept heading south, Jobs and Sculley started bickering. Until this year Jobs seemed to be the chief executive's mesmerizing alter ego. "John adored Steve," says one Apple executive. "They would finish each other's sentences." Even Sculley admits that, "like many people, I fell under the sway of Steve's charisma." But Sculley, who thinks that part of his job was to "help Steve grow as a manager," was pressuring Jobs to deliver new products on time. Jobs retorted that Sculley didn't understand the nuts and bolts of the business or how products were developed. In conversations with friends at Apple, Jobs started questioning Sculley's competence. By early April the backbiting reached a point where Sculley scolded Jobs about it. Jobs felt the dressing-down was just a "lover's quarrel." Sculley, informants make clear, felt otherwise.

The rift between the two men widened at the April 11 board meeting. For months Apple's top managers and board members had been discussing a reorganization, part of which called for bringing in a more seasoned manager to run the Mac division. At times Jobs seemed to accept the idea and had hinted he might like to run a new research-and-development operation within the company. At other times he seemed to worry that bringing in someone who had not been part of the Mac development team would sap the division's spirit. One of Jobs' lieutenants recalls that "Steve was genuinely frightened that a blue-suited marketer with an MBA wouldn't understand Mac's technological possibilities. He didn't want any bozos around whom he couldn't control."

At the board meeting, the directors urged Sculley to make it clear that he was the chief executive officer. Sculley answered that it was hard to act as a CEO when he had to boss

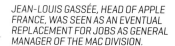

a general manager of the Mac division who happened to be chairman of the board. At a meeting unpleasant for all, the board resolved that its chairman would relinquish his Mac position. According to his friends, Jobs has not forgiven Sculley for what seemed to him a cruel surprise attack.

But nobody had set a schedule for Jobs' abdication, and in the following weeks he seemed to forget the meaning of the board's resolution. "In John's mind, it was to be a phase-out, but in Steve's it was a reprieve," says a source close to both. The difference in perception led to the final eruption.

As part of their plan to strengthen the Mac division, both Sculley and Jobs had been courting Jean-Louis Gassée, 41, head of Apple France, as an eventual replacement for Jobs. Gassée, a strong-willed and erudite mathematician who had built his own electronic calculator at the age of 14, was responsible for turning Apple France into the company's fastest-growing and most profitable foreign division. Despite his arrogance, Gassée was a respected veteran of Hewlett-Packard and Data General. Sculley planned to move Gassée into the Mac division as marketing director and make him general manager at some unspecified date, and Jobs agreed. Gassée insisted on getting a written guarantee pinning down the date of his promotion to general manager.

JOBS WAS OUTRAGED by this demand. He felt that Gassée should first prove himself in the Mac division, as other managers had. But Jobs also seems to have had second thoughts about relinquishing his own authority and about what power would be left to him if the Mac division disappeared in a restructuring. Jobs began suggesting to his friends that Apple was too small for both Sculley and himself; the board would have to choose between them.

The day after Apple announced that Gassée would become marketing manager for the Macintosh, Jobs called together his top aides—Murray, Belleville, Deborah Coleman, Mac's manufacturing director, and Susan Barnes, the controller—at the Mac building in Cupertino. Jobs asked, in a hypothetical vein, whether these managers would stick with him if forced to choose between Jobs and Sculley. They all said yes, but with more reluctance than enthusiasm.

Thus began a one-week attempt at a coup. Reportedly, Jobs had already been testing his standing in talks with some directors, as well as members of the executive committee, including Yocam, Campbell, and Jay Elliot, vice president of human resources. Though one director told him that the board was behind Sculley and that the chairman should stop being childish, Jobs apparently thought he

had a good chance to topple the chief executive. On Thursday, May 23, Jobs told his aides that Sculley wanted him out. The response was gratifying: They urged him to fight back and proposed calling the directors individually to win them over to the chairman's side.

Sculley got wind of the plot almost instantly. At a 9 a.m. meeting of the executive committee the following day, attended by Jobs, the chief executive laid bare Jobs' machinations. Sculley firmly stated that he was the one who was running Apple. In a tense roundtable discussion that lasted three hours, the committee tried to find some future role for Jobs and failed. Reportedly, Jobs maintained unusual self-control during the ordeal, while Yocam and Campbell found it excruciating, since they felt unable to speak in support of either Jobs or Sculley. At last, Jobs volunteered to take a long-planned vacation and to return after the reorganization was complete.

After his meeting with Sculley, he called his own top executives together. At 1:07 p.m., says one who noted the time, he tearfully declared that he was resigning from Apple. As he headed for the door, Barnes, also crying, rose to restrain him, and so did Coleman. Murray pleaded with Jobs not to go, saying that if he did, his life, the lives of his staff, and the history of Apple would be changed irrevocably. Belleville resigned immediately. Eventually, Jobs' aides convinced him that he still had a future at Apple.

Over Memorial Day weekend, Jobs had a long talk with Sculley and again tried—in vain—to retain some sort of operating job at Apple. That Monday night, Jobs held a dinner at his large stucco house in Woodside for Barnes, Belleville, Coleman, Murray, and board member A.C. "Mike" Markkula Jr., a former Apple president who owns 9% of the stock. Though the talk centered on Apple's business problems, Jobs seemed to be trying to sway Markkula and through him the board. Markkula, eschewing the whole-wheat pizzas being served, nibbled on some cherries. He said little, other than telling the Mac executives that the board would soon carry out a reorganization.

For Jobs, though, time had run out. The next night, sources close to Jobs say, he learned by phone from Sculley that the company's reorganization plans included absolutely no operating role for the chairman.

Sculley and his staff—Jobs didn't show—carved the new Apple in two marathon meetings on May 29 and 30. The structure, announced May 31, is almost entirely functional: Yocam runs all of Apple's engineering, manufacturing, and distribution. Gassée, who reports to Yocam, is in charge of product development. Campbell is responsible for U.S. marketing and sales. Two weeks later, Apple announced that it would permanently close three of its six factories by September and would terminate 1,200 full-time employees, including part of the field sales staff only recently hired and trained. Most security analysts estimate the company will show a pretax loss of $30 million for the quarter that ended in June and post per-share earnings for fiscal 1985, which ends on September 30, of 70 cents, vs. $1.05 last year.

Even Jobs' strongest supporters consider the new setup a plus for Apple. The company has a chance to present one face to dealers and customers. That should help especially with business prospects, who have been put off by the turmoil and the conflicting messages from rival product divisions.

Apple is following several promising paths that Jobs opposed. The great strength of the original Apple II as well as the IBM PC is that they attracted swarms of outside suppliers whose specialized add-on hardware and software vastly expanded the markets for those machines. Yet Jobs, believing that the personal computer should become as simple to use as a telephone, loaded the Mac with special software that makes it a daunting task for programmers to write new software. The Mac division had also insisted that the new machine, unlike the Apple II and IBM PC, have no slots into which outside manufacturers could slide printed circuitboards for, say, expanding the computer's memory or adding a superfast mathematical processor.

In late June, during his first public appearance since the reorganization, Sculley declared that Apple would make every effort to open up the Mac to third-party hardware and software companies. Sculley also plans to set up a group to deal with other computer companies known to be interested in using Macs as terminals for their mainframes. These manufacturers have hitherto met a confused reception at Apple, as well as occasional derision from Jobs.

One way to make the Mac more appealing to businesses is to fill out the product line with equipment they want—such as large disk drives—and with more powerful versions of the machine itself. Gassée is closemouthed about his plans, but by year-end Apple should be shipping devices that enable different Macs to share the same corporate data and programs. By next year the company will probably unveil a Mac with vastly expanded memory and the ability to accept a broader range of peripheral gear.

The other requisite for putting Macs into businesses is effective distribution. Earlier this year, partly to calm the ire of dealers, Apple throttled back its efforts to sell directly to corporations. Now Campbell is trying to help Apple dealers compete with the direct sales forces of IBM and other rivals by inundating them with technical training. He also hopes to sell Macs jointly with mainframe companies that want to hawk the machine as part of their own computer systems.

APPLE IS IN LITTLE DANGER of becoming another corpse in the personal computer wars. Though earnings are melting, the company sits on an estimated $190 million in cash and has no long-term debt. In the aftermath of Jobs' defeat, however, the company is fragile in human terms; it's quivering with threats and rumors of resignations by employees who are still loyal to the chairman. What Apple must do is hold together and carry out the latest product and marketing plans. To remain a strong contender in the long run, the company will also need the kinds of breakthrough products to which Jobs is devoted.

Though Apple hopes to retain Jobs, it's unclear whether he will stay on. In recent weeks he has seemed content to perform ambassadorial roles—promoting the Macintosh in French universities and jetting to the Soviet Union to check out opportunities for selling computers. But Jobs has also talked of selling his stock—recently worth about $120 million—to endow a new R&D outfit that he would head. If he does leave, the company will lose a champion of innovation, a foe of bureaucracy, and a priceless proselytizer to the rest of the world.

STEVE JOBS' AMAZING MOVIE ADVENTURE

DISNEY IS BETTING ON COMPUTERDOM'S EX–BOY WONDER TO DELIVER THIS YEAR'S ANIMATED CHRISTMAS BLOCKBUSTER. CAN HE DO FOR HOLLYWOOD WHAT HE DID FOR SILICON VALLEY?

BY BRENT SCHLENDER

DISNEY PIXAR

WOODY AND BUZZ STAR IN PIXAR'S TOY STORY.

ABOUT A DOZEN YEARS AGO, way back when Steve Jobs still ran Apple Computer, an irreverent underling first used the expression "reality distortion field" to describe the beguilingly rosy scenarios his boss could conjure up to push his product and business strategies. It's the kind of clever and disarming rhetoric required of promoters and dealmakers in more speculative arenas: In Hollywood and politics, they call it spin.

But in the binary business of computers, Jobs' salesmanship cuts both ways. While still in his 20s, Jobs combined it with an uncanny knack for exploiting underappreciated technologies to bring to market three of the late 20th century's watershed products: the Apple II and Macintosh personal computers and the laser printer—devices that truly have changed the way we work, learn, play, and communicate.

After he turned 30, however, Jobs' gift for hyperbole boomeranged. He wore out his welcome at Apple, bolting in 1985 after losing a nasty power struggle with John Sculley. Almost simultaneously, Jobs founded Next, vowing that the iconoclastic venture would revolutionize not only PC hardware and software, but also manufacturing technology and higher education. Alas, only now, after trying and junking a decade's worth of business plans and burning through more than $150 million from Ross Perot, Canon, and others, can Jobs truthfully claim that Next is consistently profitable. It is but a shadow of his original vision, a tiny purveyor of esoteric software whose annual revenues amount to less than a rounding error for his old nemesis, Microsoft.

Perhaps it's no wonder that Jobs has kept a low profile for the past few years, trying quietly to buff up his tarnished credibility in Silicon Valley by sticking with Next through thick and thin. Moreover, since getting married in 1991, Jobs has mellowed a little. Rather than jet off to his Manhattan penthouse to hang with the glitterati, he stays home in Palo Alto to putter around in his vegetable garden and kick back with his wife and three kids (including a teenage daughter from a previous relationship). Having turned 40, the father of the personal computer industry has traded in his black Porsche for a cherry-red Jeep Cherokee and settled into relative obscurity.

Until now. Starting this fall, the computer industry's original impresario of virtual reality will be back in your face. This time it's not a paradigm-busting computer or novel operating system Jobs is talking about. This time he's touting a new kind of movie.

No, Jobs hasn't gone Hollywood—not exactly. If anything, he's gone "Siliwood," geek shorthand for the ballyhooed "digital convergence" of Hollywood and Silicon Valley. The term is appropriate because Jobs' new movie is the world's first completely computer-animated full-length feature film. The name of the movie is *Toy Story*, and it was made by Jobs' other major investment since leaving Apple, a Bay Area computer-graphics company called Pixar.

Financed, marketed, and distributed as part of an unusual deal Jobs cut with the Walt Disney Co., *Toy Story* will play in hundreds of cinemas across America during the Thanksgiving and Christmas holiday season. Its release marks the first time Hollywood has turned to Silicon Valley not just for gee-whiz technology or a few minutes of special effects but for an entire movie—screenplay, direction, staging, filming, editing, and post-production. Disney, which coached Pixar throughout the film's four years of development and production, is marketing *Toy Story* as its year-end animated blockbuster, with licensing deals for spinoff toys and a promotional campaign at Burger King.

The film has the makings of a hit. It features the voices of Tom Hanks (he plays Woody, an old-fashioned, floppy cowboy doll) and Tim Allen (Buzz Lightyear, a plastic space-ranger action figure). These playthings, as any kid could predict, lead exciting lives when humans aren't around. They act out a classic buddy adventure, complete with jealousy, breathtaking chase sequences, and a bad guy—a 10-year-old neighbor boy who likes to blow up toys with firecrackers. But what should really grab the audience is the movie's stunning three-dimensional look. "We believe it's the biggest advance in animation since Walt Disney started it all with the release of *Snow White* 50 years ago," gushes Jobs. Adds Disney chairman Michael Eisner: "It's both a spectacular movie and a lovable movie."

Pixar's techniques so dramatically reduce the
amount of manual labor required that they may
well change the economics of animation.

THE STORY BEHIND the making of *Toy Story* is in its own right a fascinating tale of business and technology. The movie represents the splashiest of debuts for Pixar's techno-artists, some of whom have dreamed, schemed, and invented for 20 years to reach this heady moment. It also represents payday—the company plans to make its initial offering of shares to the public this winter, while the movie is in theaters.

Moreover, Pixar's animation technology is a cinematic milestone, not only because it creates a slick new 3-D look for cartoons but also because it makes possible for the first time the stockpiling of digital characters, sets, props, and even scenes. Stored in the computer, they can be reproduced and adapted economically and infinitely, in film and video sequels and spinoff products like toys, TV shows, and CD-ROM games. Pixar's techniques so dramatically reduce the amount of manual labor required to make high-quality cartoons that they may well change the economics of animation.

The release of *Toy Story* marks the beginning of a new chapter in the storied career of Steve Jobs. If the movie's a hit, he'll rub shoulders with the kingpins of the brave new world of digital entertainment—moguls like Eisner and Steven Spielberg and megastars like Hanks and Allen. Jobs may in fact have found, at last, his natural element—a business in which fantasy and technology actually enhance each other. With Pixar and *Toy Story*, the "reality" Jobs creates just might, for once, exceed his own rhapsodic rhetoric.

Point Richmond, Calif., home of Pixar's "digital backlot and studios," is an anachronism of a town clinging to a bluff on the northern shore of San Francisco Bay. A quaint working-class community that once earned its keep repairing sea vessels, Point Richmond now is known mainly for the big Chevron oil refinery across the freeway from downtown. It seems worlds away from Multimedia Gulch, the hotbed of CD-ROM development in San Francisco, or the chip plants of Silicon Valley, or Tinseltown itself, 400 miles down the coast. Yet, for now at least, Pixar's Point Richmond headquarters is the epicenter of Siliwood, a cluttered, quirky place where it's impossible to tell the difference between a computer hacker and an artist.

Jobs first heard of Pixar while still at Apple in 1984. Back then, Pixar was the computer division of Lucasfilm Ltd.—the San Rafael, Calif., outfit making George Lucas's Star Wars movies. Jobs was steered to Lucasfilm by Apple research scientist Alan Kay, whom Jobs had met a few years earlier at Xerox's famed Palo Alto Research Center, where he'd found languishing the technologies that ultimately resulted in the Macintosh and the laser printer. Lucas wanted to sell the division, and Jobs was so impressed that he tried— in vain—to persuade Apple's board to buy it.

Shortly after he left in 1985, Jobs sold all but one share of his Apple stock, raising more than $120 million. He quickly invested about $12 million in Next, but that left a lot of change jingling in his pocket. In 1986, Jobs went back to Lucas and, after haggling over the price, agreed to pay $10 million for Pixar. He briefly considered folding the Lucas team into Next, but chose instead to keep the company independent.

What did Jobs get for his money? Initially, little more than the fanciful dreams of some very smart people. Pixar was less a business than a band of idealistic researchers who for a decade had drifted like gypsies from one benefactor to another, inventing the tools of their trade along the way.

Sugar Daddy No. 1 was an eccentric millionaire named Alexander Schure, who was president of the New York Institute of Technology, more a technical school than a research university. In the early '70s, Schure had hired a team of conventional animators to turn the story from a children's record album called *Tubby the Tuba* into a movie, but was frustrated by the plodding pace and graphic limitations of conventional hand-drawn "cel animation." After hearing that the University of Utah was pioneering a new field called computer graphics, he flew in 1974 to Salt Lake City, hoping to find a whiz kid who could automate the making of *Tubby*. The kid Schure found was an unassuming computer scientist named Ed Catmull, a native of Utah who had dreamed his whole life of making cartoons, despite the fact that he couldn't draw well at all.

Catmull, now Pixar's executive vice president and chief technical officer, assembled a team of artistically inclined techies. For four years on the institute's Long Island campus, they tinkered with what at the time was the largest concentration of computer-graphics equipment on the East Coast. They didn't make *Tubby*, but some of them did produce works of video art. One of these, *Sunstone*, was acquired by New York City's Museum of Modern Art.

Although Catmull and company were pleased with their progress, they had no qualms about leaving Schure in 1979, when George Lucas, fresh from his *Star Wars* success, offered to bring them to Northern California as part of Lucasfilm. He wanted Catmull's team to design computerized equipment for combining, editing, and printing film images, and to produce special effects for his movies. Recalls Alvy Ray Smith, an early Pixarian who's now a research fellow at Microsoft: "Lucas wasn't interested in computer animation per se, but with all his glamour, it was easy for us to hire the best people in the business. We built all the machines he wanted in a few years, and he thought we were done, but we were only getting started."

Through the early '80s, Catmull made annual pilgrimages to computer graphics conferences to show off the team's work. There he made friends with a gifted young animator from Disney named John Lasseter, who had worked on *Tron*, a live-action adventure (and box-office bomb) that was Disney's first major try at computerized special effects. Lasseter had studied animation at the California Institute of the Arts, where one of his classmates was Tim Burton, the director of *Batman* and *Edward Scissorhands*. In 1984, Lasseter came up to Lucasfilm to work with the computer division for a month. He never went back. Now Pixar's vice president for creative development, he directed *Toy Story*.

That same year, Lucas began to shop the division around. Catmull still shudders when he recalls that at one point Lucas nearly arranged to sell to a partnership of General Motors' EDS computer services company and a unit of Dutch electronics conglomerate Philips NV. When Jobs came calling, however, Catmull and company dared to hope that they'd finally found a kindred spirit who would set them free creatively.

Pixar's hallways are lined with huge bulletin boards like those found at any animation studio; each is covered with dozens of hand-sketched scenes that story editors arrange and rearrange *until they settle on a sequence. Says the vice president for feature films production, Ralph Guggenheim: "One beauty of the animation process is that it's the equivalent of editing before you shoot. We save a lot of film that way."*

What makes Pixar animation different from the traditional kind is that characters, props, and sets aren't drawings but three-dimensional mathematical models stored in the computer. On screen, they take up space, cast shadows, and can be manipulated as if they were real. Something big like a room or a car can be created using computer-aided-design programs much like those that architects and engineers employ. Trees are drawn on the computer by artists. The shapes of characters and small objects are fed into the machine with the help of a special pen that plots coordinates on the surface of a physical object or sculpted clay model. Bill Reeves, Pixar's technical director, devised much of the necessary software and is one of the company's most proficient "modelers." What is the most difficult object he's ever undertaken? A hand.

"If I knew in 1986 how much it was going to cost to keep Pixar going, I doubt if I would have bought the company," admits Jobs. "The problem was, for many years the cost of the computers required to make animation we could sell was tremendously high. Only in the past few years has the price come down to the point that it makes business sense."

LOUIE PSIHOYOS—CORBIS

Since Jobs didn't buy Pixar intending to subsidize it forever, he insisted that Catmull and crew put off their ultimate goal—to make cartoons and movies—and develop salable technical products. The first was a piece of software called RenderMan, which enables computer-graphics artists to apply textures and colors to surfaces of 3-D objects onscreen. The Silicon Graphics workstations that generated the frighteningly realistic dinosaurs for *Jurassic Park* relied on RenderMan to create the creatures' scaly skin and ivory teeth. Pixar has sold about 100,000 copies of RenderMan, which was for many years the company's main source of revenue.

Disney was the second source of sales. Pixar created a software system called CAPS (short for computer-animation production system) that helped Disney animators streamline the conventional animation process and juice up their special effects.

N TIME, IT BECAME CLEAR that RenderMan, CAPS, and other ventures—like manufacturing computer-graphics hardware—were never going to pay Pixar's bills. Jobs decided that the company should concentrate on developing content: short films and TV commercials. Some Pixar ads are memorable. A series for Listerine includes one spot in which the trademark mouthwash bottle comes to life as Robin Hood and another in which the bottle becomes General Patton. Pixar's ads have won two Clio awards.

Still, the company has never turned a profit. While Jobs won't cite a dollar figure, he acknowledges that he has invested more money in Pixar than in Next. Others at Pixar estimate he has pumped in nearly $50 million. As recently as last year, Jobs wasn't sure he could continue carrying the venture, and quietly sent out feelers—to Microsoft, among other companies—to see what kind of price Pixar might bring. Only after Disney committed to distributing *Toy Story* for the 1995 holiday season did he decide to hang on.

"Let's return Mr. Potato Head's facial features to the default position, so it's easier for the baby to bite off his nose," suggests John Lasseter, as he leans over an animator's shoulder to study a two-second shot of a toddler torturing her toy. "And let's see if we can make the baby's slobber more elastic, so it sticks and stretches longer." Director Lasseter is on his daily walk-through of the animators' lair, an eerie open office lit only by glowing computer monitors and a few halogen desk lamps. A swing hangs from a crossbeam in the ceiling. Each animator's carrel looks like a shrine to a favorite toy. It is here that Lasseter helps the animators fine-tune the action of the movie. "At Pixar, an animator is more an actor than an artist," he explains. "Sure, they can draw,

but the real trick is to make these 3-D characters come to life. That requires acting ability more than anything else."

Until work on *Toy Story* geared up in 1991, Pixar employed only a few dozen people, and Lasseter was practically the only bona fide animator on the payroll. He split his time between advising software engineers about the tools animators would need and making demo films that showcased Pixar's evolving technology. The demos displayed Lasseter's genius as an animator. He brought to life such inanimate objects as a desk lamp, a unicycle, tacky souvenirs, and, of course, toys, in whimsical ways envied even by the animators at Disney. One film, *Tin Toy*, won an Oscar in 1988.

The shorts also showed off the growing flexibility of Pixar's animation system. Characters, sets, and props resurfaced in one film after another. Such efficiencies helped Pixar make *Toy Story* with a staff of just 110—roughly one-sixth the number Disney and others employ to make an animated feature. Disney hopes to use similar processes to cut the number of animators on its own projects.

Each day about mid-morning, Lasseter presides over "the lighting meeting," the final, crucial step before scenes are released to be transferred from the computer onto actual film. Lasseter and his lighting specialists watch a handful of shots over and over again on the computer screen, trying to imagine how the lighting would work in the real world. Even after a shot is created, techies can simulate the look of adding extra lights from different angles to bring out the features of 3-D characters and props. They can even create "lens flare," the glinty effect of a camera lens accidentally aiming at a light source. Today, Lasseter is studying the refraction properties of raindrops on a window. "Each drop is a lens and should reflect everything that's going on outside," he says. "You should be able to see the moving van pulling up outside in miniature in each of these drops. Let's add 50 more so people won't miss the effect."

In 1991, Lasseter felt the Pixar technology was robust enough to make an hour-long computer-animated TV special. He pitched the idea to Disney, hoping the big studio would help fund the project. Jeffrey Katzenberg, who was running Eisner's film business, was already enamored of Lasseter's style. (Now a principal of DreamWorks, Katzenberg contends that the director is Pixar's biggest asset.) Katzenberg and Eisner came back with an unexpected counteroffer: How about making a full-scale movie that Disney would pay for and distribute? Not surprisingly, Jobs, who'd been absorbed by the trials and tribulations at Next, suddenly started paying more attention to his other company. He got involved in the negotiations with Disney and hired one of Hollywood's most respected entertainment lawyers to help hammer out a deal. The result was a contract for Pixar to make three feature films. Disney would pick up most of the production and promotion costs, as long as it had complete control over marketing and licensing the films and their characters. Pixar would create the screenplays and the visual style for each picture and receive a percentage of the box-office gross revenues and video sales.

It seemed like a great deal at the time, and Jobs still isn't really complaining. But he now realizes that much of the profit from a successful animated film comes via ancillary merchandise—and Pixar doesn't get a cent of those revenues. Says Jobs: "If *Toy Story* is a modest hit—say $75 million at the box office—we'll both break even. If it gets $100 million, we'll both make money. But if it's a real blockbuster and earns $200 million or so at the box office, we'll make good money, and Disney will make a lot of money."

GIVEN THE EGOS INVOLVED, one might wonder if the Jobs-Eisner relationship has its tense moments. No, says Jobs, not yet: "You've got to believe there's some truth to Disney's reputation for being hard to deal with, but we haven't experienced that. We have found that we share the same values. We are as much perfectionists as they are. We both believe that if you produce the best-quality story and movie that you can, the rest will take care of itself, and so far it has."

Eisner too seems smitten with the movie and happy with the relationship. "I don't think either side thought *Toy Story* would turn out as well as it has. The technology is brilliant, the casting is inspired, and I think the story will touch a nerve. Believe me, when we first agreed to work together, we never thought their first movie would be our 1995 holiday feature, or that they could go public on the strength of it."

All gushing aside, there's still rivalry between the two companies, at least from Pixar's point of view. Employees have set up a betting pool to predict how *Toy Story* will stack up against *Pocahontas* at the box office. For what it's worth, most wagers have recently turned in favor of *Toy Story*.

At 8:30 each morning, people start filing into Pixar's screening room for a meeting at which Lasseter reviews the final versions of shots and scenes that Pixar's "farm" of 300 Sun Microsystems computers has rendered onto film. There's often a standing-room-only crowd when an especially popular scene is projected in full 35mm glory. If Lasseter gives the final okay, the scenes are spliced into the master reel. Once in the can, Toy

Story will have more than 1,500 different shots and about 110,000 individual frames, each of which requires two to five hours of computer time to transfer onto film.

While *Toy Story* is only now moving into the public eye, much of Pixar's 150-person staff has already gone on to other projects. A story team is working on the script and general design for the company's second feature—Jobs isn't saying what it's about. Another team is creating *Toy Story* CD-ROM games. Yet another group just finished three new Coca-Cola commercials that were commissioned by Michael Ovitz, the head of Creative Artists Agency and soon-to-be president of Disney. Says Jobs: "Can you believe our luck? He loves the commercials we made, and now we'll be working with him on our movies."

MEANWHILE, executive vice president and chief financial officer Lawrence Levy is readying Pixar's initial public offering. Jobs, who owns 75% of the company (employees own the rest), is helping him line up a board of directors. So far, Joseph Graziano, executive vice president and CFO of Apple Computer, Skip Brittenham, Pixar's Hollywood lawyer, and Larry Sonsini, a prominent Silicon Valley attorney, have agreed to serve. Intel CEO Andy Grove reluctantly declined.

Even as Jobs promotes Pixar and *Toy Story*, he hints that Next may also go public soon. His wife, Laurene, gave birth in mid-August to their second child, a girl. With all this activity, Jobs seems stretched about as thin as any 40-year-old CEO should ever get. Is there anything else he would possibly take on right now? "You know, I've got a plan that could rescue Apple," he says, in all seriousness. "I can't say any more than that it's the perfect product and the perfect strategy for Apple. But nobody there will listen to me ..."

The big question, of course, is "What will kids think of Toy Story?" *To find out, I took my two daughters, Fernanda and Greta, ages 9 and 10, to Jobs' home to join his 3-year-old son, Reed, for an unofficial screening. Reed's attention wanders, but my kids are transfixed, even though about 30% of this cut is in black-and-white storyboard form rather than in full-motion 3-D animation. When it's over, Jobs waits all of three seconds before asking, "So, whaddya think, is it as good as* Pocahontas?" *Greta and Fernanda, both of whom saw the Disney blockbuster the weekend before, nod vigorously. "Well, then," he asks, "is it as good as* The Lion King?" *Fernanda puts her chin in her hand to ponder this one, and then gives Jobs an answer that makes his day: "To tell you the truth, I won't really be able to make up my mind until I see* Toy Story *five or six more times."*

LOUIE PSIHOYOS—CORBIS

WHERE IT ALL BEGAN: JOBS IN FRONT OF HIS FAMILY'S GARAGE IN PALO ALTO IN 1996, 20 YEARS AFTER LAUNCHING APPLE THERE. **PHOTOGRAPH BY DIANE COOK & LEN JENSHEL**

CONTOUR BY GETTY

Chapter Three

THE RETURN TO APPLE

These stories chronicled Jobs' return to Apple in 1997. A series of CEOs had driven the computer maker into the red, causing a worried board to call Jobs back from exile to run the company. Starting with the iMac and the iPod, Jobs began launching a series of hit consumer products that turned Apple's fortunes around and made him once again the favorite bad boy of Silicon Valley.

The Legacy of Steve Jobs

Chapter Three

David Strick

Fortune
March 3,
1997

SOMETHING'S ROTTEN IN CUPERTINO

AS CEO GIL AMELIO AND AN INEFFECTUAL BOARD DITHERED, APPLE COMPUTER LOST MARKET SHARE AND FADED INTO INSIGNIFICANCE. NOW STEVE JOBS HAS RETURNED WITH A TURNAROUND STRATEGY THAT COULD MAKE APPLE HIS ONCE AGAIN.

BY BRENT SCHLENDER

Two years of woe
for Apple and its
shareholders

Things were bad under Michael Spindler, the CEO who left in February 1996. Under Gil Amelio, the situation has deteriorated. Despite a blip of profitability in the fourth quarter of fiscal 1996, Apple is, on the whole, a money-losing venture whose sales are tanking while the share price falls toward an all-time low.

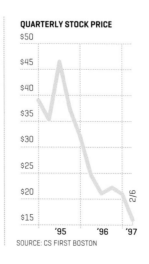

QUARTERLY STOCK PRICE
$50
$45
$40
$35
$30
$25
$20
$15
2/6
'95   '96   '97

SOURCE: CS FIRST BOSTON

SALES ($ BILLION)
$3.25
$3.00
$2.75
$2.50
$2.25
$2.00
$1.75
Est.
'95   '96   '97

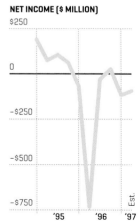

NET INCOME ($ MILLION)
$250
0
-$250
-$500
-$750
Est.
'95   '96   '97

REDUX

SCOTT MANCHESTER—SYGMA/CORBIS

HERE WE GO AGAIN. Apple Computer, Silicon Valley's paragon of dysfunctional management and fumbled techno-dreams, is back in crisis mode, scrambling lugubriously in slow motion to deal with imploding sales, a floundering technology strategy, and a hemorrhaging brand name. About all that Apple's 13,000 shell-shocked employees, its 30,000 hapless shareholders, and the 20 million queasy Macintosh faithful can do is look on in dismay, just as the company's chronically passive board seems to be doing once again. In January, Wall Street joined the crowd, horrified by results announced for the quarter that ended December 27. Apple's sales had plummeted by a frightening 32%, to just $2.1 billion, creating a stunning $120 million loss.

As they tried to glean hope from CEO Gil Amelio's vague public pronouncements, onlookers had no way of knowing that, for all the apparent turmoil, what's going on behind the scenes is even weirder. At Apple's headquarters in Cupertino, Calif., a power play is in progress that calls into question who's really running the company and that may very well put Apple in play once again. So thick is this plot that it reaches into the homes of some of the most powerful CEOs in Silicon Valley. The delicious irony is that what triggered the soap opera is a move Amelio hopes is his masterstroke: Apple's $400 million acquisition of Next and the advisory services of Steve Jobs that come bundled with it.

Amelio's big deal is beginning to look more like a Next takeover of Apple. Never mind that Next Software was a boutique with revenues that would amount to less than a rounding error to Apple. Jobs, the Svengali of Silicon Valley, may have outdone himself this time: Not only did he collect $100 million and 1.5 million shares of Apple stock for his stake in Next, but his fingerprints are all over Amelio's latest reorganization plan and product strategy—even though Jobs doesn't have an operational role or even a board seat.

To the Machiavellian eye, it looks as if Jobs, despite the lure of Hollywood—lately he has been overseeing Pixar, maker of *Toy Story* and other computer-animated films—might be scheming to take over Apple for himself. If anyone doubts he could do it, all you have to do is ask his best friend, Oracle CEO Larry Ellison, the richest man in Silicon Valley. Says he: "Steve's the only one who can save Apple. We've talked about it very seriously many, many times, and I'm ready to help him the minute he says the word. I could raise the money in a week."

Ellison, who concedes he sometimes makes outrageous

statements "just to be provocative," could be blowing smoke. But Jobs has never completely severed the emotional ties to his first and greatest creation. Anybody who knows him well will tell you that rarely a day goes by when he doesn't think about what he would do if he were running Apple.

Amelio told us, "Apple is a boat. There's a hole in the boat, and it's taking on water. But there's also a treasure on board. And the problem is, everyone on board is rowing in different directions, so the boat is just standing still. My job is to get everyone rowing in the same direction so we can save the treasure."

After he turned away, I looked at the person next to me and asked, "But what about the hole?"

—A Silicon Valley CEO recalling Amelio's description of his task at Apple during a cocktail party in spring 1996

CHAOS REIGNED IN CUPERTINO in February of last year, when the board handed Amelio, a director since 1994, the keys to Apple. For two months, his predecessor, Michael Spindler, had been trying frantically to sell Apple to two potential suitors—Sun Microsystems, the hot Unix workstation maker, and Philips, the Dutch consumer electronics giant. Spindler had turned to them after a futile three-year effort to bring IBM to the altar. Mac sales were in a steep decline, due largely to bad forecasting and production problems.

According to Apple board insiders, as early as December 1995 another director—Spindler appointee Jurgen Hintz, a former Procter & Gamble executive—had volunteered to take over. Amelio, meanwhile, started quietly lobbying directors to give him the job. Spindler's fate was sealed when the merger talks fell apart in January amid a storm of financial bad news and mistaken newspaper reports about the terms and likelihood of the potential Sun deal. When the board acted, it did so in a highly unusual fashion, hiring Amelio without conducting an executive search.

Amelio brought a reputation as a turnaround artist. He outlined his philosophy in *Profit From Experience*, a book chronicling his deeds at National Semiconductor. It es-

←

WHO'S IN CHARGE HERE? GIL AMELIO
LACKS THE CHARISMA OF STEVE JOBS.

pouses an approach Amelio calls "transformation management"; his fellow directors hoped he would put his tactics right to work.

Recalls Amelio, "When I walked in the door, I was facing five crises: We were dangerously low on cash; the quality of our products was poor; the development of our next generation [software] was behind schedule and in disarray; Apple's famously contrarian corporate culture was almost impossible to manage; and our product line and development efforts were fragmented to the point that the company was completely unfocused."

The new CEO took immediate action on the financial front, bringing in a CFO, Fred Anderson from Automatic Data Processing, the Roseland, N.J., computer-services company. They cleaned up the balance sheet by writing off inventories, and hastily pulled together a new business plan. It assumed that Apple's weakening revenues would stop falling once annual sales had shrunk to $9 billion, from $11.1 billion in fiscal 1995. (Apple's fiscal year ends in September.) To maintain a gross margin of 20%, Apple announced that it would cut costs and eliminate 2,800 of its 17,000 jobs. All this became grim reality by the time Apple announced March-quarter results. Net sales slipped 18% to $2.2 billion; Apple took big charges for inventory write-downs and restructuring, resulting in a lurid $740 million net loss.

Amelio started addressing the quality crisis in the June quarter, recalling a line of balky Macs. He also firmed up his management team.

That's where the cracks in his recovery plan started to show. Aside from Anderson, Amelio's lieutenants all hailed from the semiconductor industry. Two—George Scalise, who heads operations, and chief technologist Ellen Hancock, a former IBM heavyweight—were colleagues from National Semiconductor. Amelio also elevated Marco Landi, a Texas Instruments veteran who had joined Apple in 1995 as head of European operations.

Neither Amelio nor the others had substantial experience in the PC business. While the chip business is a process-oriented industry that churns out discrete components, the PC business is more like a cross between Procter & Gamble and Bell Labs. It entails the design of complex systems in which software and hardware components from dozens of suppliers must mesh perfectly. Customer relationships differ too. The typical chip buyer is a purchasing agent for an electronics manufacturer—someone to do business with on the golf course. Apple's core customers, by contrast, are fickle consumers.

Inexperience helps explain why Amelio has had such a tough time addressing the other crises he spoke of, and why the company's products and sales and marketing efforts still seem chaotic. Apple appeared to find its legs in the fiscal fourth quarter ended in September, when it posted a $25 million net profit, largely as the result of reversed restructuring charges and a flurry of last-minute shipments. Still, sales slipped 23%, to $2.3 billion. At that rate of erosion, Amelio's $9-billion-a-year breakeven target began to look like a fantasy.

Apple insiders also say Amelio and his team were slow to see that managing at Apple is more art than science. "Gil seemed to think that management training would take care of most operational problems," says a senior staffer. "He set up training sessions for mid-level managers that would end up canceled because business was in disarray. He also assumed that if he issued an order, things would get done. But it doesn't work that way here."

Amelio acknowledges that passive/aggressiveness often prevails: "Apple's culture has a contrarian nature that goes right back to its founding. There are some positive aspects— we got twice as many patents last year as Microsoft, as an illustration. But the negative is that when you're in a little bit of trouble, it's a lot harder to herd the cats."

Another senior official says that Amelio has shown little sense of urgency. "It's as if Gil was a microprocessor running at 25 megahertz when the rest of the industry, and many people in Apple, have clock speeds of 200 megahertz. He takes six weeks to make a decision that should take only one. The net result is that he is slowing down other decisions that people are itching to act on. The critical resource for Apple now isn't cash or brains, but time."

All through the fall, Amelio and Hancock dithered over what to do about Apple's chronically delayed next-generation Macintosh operating system, endlessly debating whether to license technology from Sun or Microsoft or buy a company like Be Inc., a startup run by Jean-Louis Gassée, Apple's onetime technology czar.

Hancock liked the idea of linking with Sun, especially since the two companies are Silicon Valley neighbors and have complementary product lines. Landi preferred to connect with Microsoft, figuring that an alliance would help leverage the Apple brand in the market for conventional Wintel PCs. But Amelio couldn't decide, prompting independent developers of Mac applications to worry that he might never offer a sense of direction. Says Heidi Roizen, Apple's point person for dealing with the developers: "Our developers were getting really impatient. We

JOBS WOWED THE APPLE FAITHFUL
WITH HIS PRESENTATION AT
MACWORLD IN SAN FRANCISCO.

hadn't lost many, but more were putting more emphasis on Windows work than on Mac applications, and that was really beginning to hurt."

Meanwhile, the financial picture was bleak. U.S. retailers had stocked too many low-end Macs at the end of that profitable September quarter. Not even sharp price cuts could move them off the shelves. By Thanksgiving, it was clear Apple's Christmas quarter would be a disaster. Moreover, Macworld, the annual confab of Apple faithful, was set for January, and Amelio had to have a new operating-system strategy or lose all credibility. It was time to act. As if on cue, Steve Jobs entered the picture.

Here's how Steve views the current situation at Apple: It's as if Apple is an old fiancée from college that Steve met again at a 20-year class reunion. Steve is happily married now with children, and has a great life. When he meets his old girlfriend again, she's an alcoholic and is running around with a bad crowd and has made a mess of her life. Even so, in his mind's eye, he still sees the beautiful woman he once thought was the love of his life. So what's he supposed to do? Of course, he doesn't want to marry her anymore, but he can't just walk away, because he still cares about her. So he puts her in a detox program and tries to help her meet a better class of friends and hopes for the best.
—Larry Ellison, CEO of Oracle

STEVE JOBS MAY BE BRASH and impulsive, but he is also stubborn. While he abruptly sold all but one of his Apple shares after being ousted in 1985, he invested some of the resulting $100 million–plus in two startups that he has stuck with through many, many lean years—Next and Pixar.

In both cases, perseverance paid. In 1995, during the smash run of *Toy Story*, the world's first full-length computer-animated film, he took Pixar public and briefly joined the rarefied ranks of Silicon Valley billionaires. (The stock peaked at $40 during its first week, then fell back to the teens, where it remains. Jobs' stake currently is worth $450 million.) "Ask about Pixar and I'll talk all day," he said recently, as he refused to grant an interview about what he's up to at Apple.

Next was a problem child. Started as a builder of computer systems, Next developed a distinctive, black desktop machine that looked as exotic as the software inside. But the hardware, which was incompatible with IBM PCs, flopped: In over four years, Next shipped just 50,000 units. In 1993,

KIM KULISH—CORBIS

"I'm giving Gil the best advice I know, and I'll keep doing so until he stops listening or tells me to go away." —Steve Jobs

Jobs laid off half his employees and refocused Next on software for Intel-based machines and Sun workstations. Since then, revenues have hovered around $50 million a year, and Next has posted an annual profit just once.

Why didn't Jobs pull the plug? It's simple—he treasures his reputation. Over the years, he told friends he feared he would never again be able to rustle up financing for any future "insanely great" idea if Next failed. It was as though Next was a 30-year-old son with a Ph.D. who was still living at home. Other CEOs say Jobs shopped the company around Silicon Valley for years.

Then along came Apple. Last October newspapers reported that it was in discussions to acquire Be, which had a nifty, if untested, operating system that could run on Mac hardware.

Jobs has told friends he wasn't even trying to sell Next to Apple when he first contacted Hancock in November. He called to urge her to steer clear of Be—he thought its software was all wrong for Apple. Hancock invited him to visit Amelio to make his case.

By the time Jobs showed up in the CEO's office in the first week of December, he had raised his sights. Rather than simply bash Be, he pitched Next as an alternative. What he ultimately offered Amelio was a whole new strategy built around Next.

Jobs claimed that Next, not Be, had the software to shore up the Macintosh. What's more, he said, Next technology would enable Apple to make Mac software work on standard PCs, which in turn would let Apple tap into a much larger potential market.

Apparently Jobs was at his charismatic best. Just one week later, the board gave Amelio the go-ahead to try to strike a deal with Jobs. On December 20, the companies came to terms. Apple agreed to buy Next for $377.5 million in cash, plus 1.5 million Apple shares, then worth about $22.5 million, that went to Jobs. In under a month, Jobs had clinched the kind of deal Apple had been considering for nearly 10 years.

Jobs has told friends that he offered to serve on the board, but that Amelio demurred. Amelio knew, however, that having the golden-tongued founder around might boost morale. The CEO proposed that Jobs become his special adviser, and Jobs agreed. Perhaps he could help his old girlfriend after all.

I'm giving Gil the best advice I know, and I'll keep doing so until he stops listening or tells me to go away.
—Steve Jobs

On January 7, when Jobs appeared with Amelio at Macworld in San Francisco to tout the Next-Apple marriage, their speeches were a study in contrasts. Jobs, garbed in a svelte Eisenhower jacket, delivered a crisp and entertaining demo of Next's operating system, explaining why it was just what the doctor ordered.

Amelio, looking uncomfortably pseudo-casual in a sport jacket and banded-collar shirt, hadn't bothered to practice his speech. He rambled. Occasionally he stopped to show off arcane software from Apple's labs. He droned on for hours.

To be sure, the CEO had a lot on his mind. Just four days before, Apple had let the world know just how awful its Christmas quarter had been, hinting that sales would decline at least 30% from the year-earlier quarter, and that net losses would exceed $100 million. Amelio also knew he'd soon have to devise yet another restructuring plan, lopping at least $400 million from the company's budgets to get the breakeven point down to $8 billion. That, of course, would mean more layoffs.

After Macworld, Jobs visited or phoned Amelio several times a week, associates say. He apparently advised Amelio not only on how to integrate Next people and products into Apple, but also on how to cut costs and redraw the organization chart.

Although Hancock had been Jobs' first contact at Apple, their relationship quickly grew rancorous. Even after the Next deal, Hancock pressed Amelio to dump Next's operating system and replace it with Sun's Solaris. Several Apple insiders say Jobs was incensed by the suggestion.

Amelio sided with Jobs. Not only did he opt to focus solely on the Next technology, but he also sharply curtailed Hancock's responsibilities. When the reorganization was announced Feb. 4, most people who had reported to Hancock got two new bosses: Next chief engineer Avie Tevanian took over software engineering, and Jon Rubinstein, who'd once headed Next's hardware unit, took over hardware engineering. Others had their wings clipped as well. Chief operating officer Landi was stripped of marketing and operations responsibilities and left in charge of Apple's worldwide sales.

Jobs also helped Amelio compile a "Hit List" and "Hot List" of product-development and cost-cutting priorities. Among other things, Jobs suggested that Amelio dump the Newton handheld computer, a John Sculley favorite that last year lost at least $40 million. Amelio says only that eliminating Newton is "on the table."

Altogether, the Hit List calls for cutting R&D by 33%,

or $200 million, and sales, general, and administrative costs by 9%, or $260 million. The cuts seem to anticipate a breakeven point of around $7.5 billion. Among the top priorities on the Hot List: development of Pentium-based Apple computers that will be able to run both Windows and the next-generation Macintosh operating system (code-named Rhapsody).

Already Apple seems sensitive to the suggestion that Jobs is wielding power. Director and former chairman Mike Markkula, while welcoming Jobs' return, downplays his influence on the reorganization. And Apple recently announced it had asked its other co-founder, Steve Wozniak, to join Jobs as an adviser to Amelio. That appointment, however, is largely cosmetic—"Woz," as he is called, spends most of his time teaching in a Silicon Valley high school.

Why do I feel like it's my fiduciary responsibility to see a negative story about my own company?
—A senior Apple official

IS APPLE REALLY ANY BETTER OFF with Jobs and Next? There are a few bright spots. Apple is readying a host of new products, including a high-powered laptop, an inexpensive network server, and a supercharged workstation. Also coming are cheap plug-in cards to make Macs compatible with Windows PCs. Moreover, the operating-system strategy seems to be settled. Ironically, it's an approach very similar to Microsoft's: Rhapsody will target power users and the network-server market, much like WindowsNT, while traditional Mac software will be sold to schools and consumers, like Windows 95.

But Apple still faces daunting problems. Morale has never been lower, and many of the best employees are leaving. Amelio hasn't helped matters by seeming to blame the troops for Apple's problems. In a broadcast to employees, as he reviewed the woeful first-quarter numbers and announced the likelihood of more layoffs and cost cutting, he stopped at one point, stared into the camera, and said, "Don't put me in this position again, dammit."

Worse, Apple has lost the confidence of its customers, and its woes are turning off potential buyers. Landi concedes that in recent quarters only a tiny portion of Mac sales have been to first-time buyers.

Apple's worst enemy is time. It must shore up its position before it runs out of cash. At the end of December, the company still had $1.8 billion in cash, but nearly $400 million of that will go to Next's shareholders, and layoffs will likely consume a considerable sum. Analysts expect the company to post a loss next quarter, which will deplete the hoard even further.

The key question now is: "Where's the bottom?" According to internal projections, the company anticipates a $1.7 billion second quarter. While it's hard to predict annual sales from any one quarter, Apple may be headed for a $7 billion year. Sales were $11 billion just two years ago.

While Amelio states publicly that Apple might break even by the fourth quarter, pessimists say the company could well run low on cash by then—and who knows what that would trigger?

For now, Apple isn't looking for a sugar daddy. Sun is no longer interested in buying the company, although it remains willing to work out a technology partnership.

A lot of Apple employees, however, are hoping that Jobs and his pal Larry Ellison will ride to the rescue. Jobs and Ellison almost made a run at Apple last year, around the time the Sun and Philips merger talks collapsed. According to Ellison, he was ready to go, but Steve balked because he didn't want to take on Apple as a full-time job just as Pixar was starting to be fun.

Ellison says the two even have a technology plan, which involves building ultra-cheap Macs and selling networks of the devices to schools, small businesses, and perhaps even consumers. Jobs, however, has said he really, really doesn't want to run Apple again—he loves what he's doing with Pixar. Fine. But consider the position he's in, and what he's done in the few weeks since Apple bought Next. First of all, of course, there's the fact that Larry Ellison, his rich, rich friend, has publicly declared he'd bankroll a Jobs takeover. Then there's the power play Jobs has run on Ellen Hancock, an industry veteran close to Amelio, who's essentially been replaced with Next veterans Tevanian and Rubinstein. Then there's the board, that passive group of mostly inexperienced observers. In the past year, two veterans have left—Hintz and venture capitalist Peter Crisp. Aside from Markkula, the board now boasts one year of collective experience in the PC industry—Amelio's reign at Apple. This crew is unlikely to push for a change as drastic as asking Jobs to replace Amelio. Other boards might, but not this one. While it stands by, Apple looks more and more like a corpse.

If the situation doesn't improve, Jobs may feel that he has to make a move. Yet Ellison thinks there's only about a 30% chance that he and Jobs will team up to take over Apple. "It's totally up to Steve," he says. "I wouldn't think of doing it without him. But you never know. Steve may not want to marry his old girlfriend, but he might just be willing to save her life."

Her pulse is getting weak.

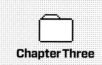

STEVIE WONDER GETS WAY COOLER
MR. APPLE'S MISSION: TO MARRY THE iMAC AND THE INTERNET WITH AN EASY-TO-USE NEW OPERATING SYSTEM AND FREE WEB SERVICES FOR EVERYTHING FROM YOUR PHOTOS TO YOUR HOMEPAGE. IF IT WORKS, MICROSOFT, AOL, AND OTHERS WILL BE PLAYING CATCH-UP WITH A COMPANY LEFT FOR DEAD TWO YEARS AGO.
BY BRENT SCHLENDER

At a Recharged Apple, the Numbers All Click

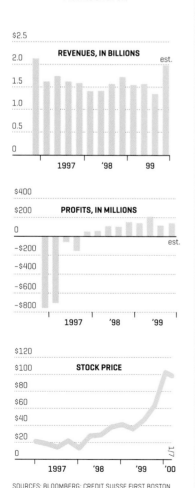

The second Jobs administration began in fall 1997; revenues remained solid, profits rebounded, and the stock is on a roll.

REVENUES, IN BILLINGS

PROFITS, IN MILLIONS

STOCK PRICE

SOURCES: BLOOMBERG; CREDIT SUISSE FIRST BOSTON

STEVE JOBS, the personal-computer industry's chief aesthetic officer, is in his element. Here in the boardroom at Apple Computer's Cupertino, Calif., headquarters, he's the only person seated. Reclining, actually. Hands clasped behind his head, he stares pokerfaced at a couple of web pages displayed side by side on an outsized 22-inch-wide Apple Cinema flat-panel monitor. Twelve weary-looking men—programmers, marketers, graphic designers, and web experts—stand in pensive poses, forming an arc behind him, some scribbling notes on Palm handheld devices whenever the 44-year-old iCEO comments.

"The icon for 'real estate' doesn't do anything for me at all," announces Jobs, snapping out of his reverie and leaning forward. He points at a web-link button on the mocked-up homepage for iReviews, Apple's new website-rating service. "That's not what a FOR SALE sign looks like. And I don't much like this 'investing'

TIME LIFE PICTURES/GETTY

icon either. I can't tell if it's supposed to look like a dollar bill or a stock certificate. But this old-fashioned highway sign for 'cars'—now that's cool. I love it! You instantly know exactly what it means."

Jobs has been presiding over secret meetings like this several hours a day, three or four times a week, throughout most of November and December. No detail was too trivial to escape his scrutiny as he passed final judgment on the look and feel—or what he calls the fit and finish—of a series of ambitious Apple software products and Internet initiatives that he would announce in early January at the annual Macworld trade show in San Francisco. These surprise announcements would prove more than the latest manifestations of Jobs' knack for high-tech showmanship. They would be his way of drawing a new line in the sand and daring Microsoft or Compaq or AOL or Sun or any other competitor to cross it.

Everyone expected him to unveil a new computer or two. Instead, Jobs showed off a flashy, completely redesigned Macintosh operating system called Mac OS X, which, when it's delivered this summer, will put a glossy new face—graphical user interface, that is—on the Mac. "We made the buttons on the screen look so good you'll want to lick them," he says. Just as provocative was a set of jazzy and useful free Internet services available immediately—online data-storage space, build-'em-yourself personal homepages and websites, and a new kind of parental-control filter to keep kids from seeing the wrong kinds of web content, to name just a few. These web services, which Apple calls iTools, are designed to work exclusively with Macintosh computers, not PCs or any other kind of Internet device. Jobs' shrewd goal: to use the Internet to make Apple's computers show up Wintel PCs rather than merely stay even.

YEP. ONCE AGAIN STEVE JOBS is trying to win by design—to use aesthetics and finesse instead of brute force to change the rules of the computing game. That's what he did when he rolled out the first Macintosh in 1984. He did it again upon returning to Apple in 1997, when he coaxed engineers to come up with the sleek, colorful iMacs and iBooks, winsome machines that consumers are buying hand over fist. Now he has turned his connoisseur's eye beyond the box, hoping that a fresh approach to system software and especially to the Internet will further fuel demand for Apple's products.

And, oh, there's a soap opera subtext to all this. Most of these software and web innovations spring from the technologies and engineers that Apple acquired in 1997 when it bought Next, the company Jobs started in a fit of pique after being cast

out of Apple in 1985. Until Apple handed over $400 million for Next, that company's software breakthroughs had been widely praised, but its products had never made much of a splash in the market. Many people thought Jobs snookered Apple's then CEO, Gil Amelio, in the deal, collecting an inflated price for Next, not to mention inveigling himself into a position to commandeer Apple if Amelio stumbled.

Now it's looking like a pretty good deal all around. (Unless you're Amelio, of course.) After being repotted into Apple along with Jobs, the Next technology has had a chance to blossom. Says Jobs: "Once this all plays out, I think we'll all feel vindicated—those of us from Next and everybody at Apple too."

STEVE HAS GOOD REASON to feel vindicated already. In four of the past five quarters, his $6-billion-a-year company has posted solid revenue gains, and it is expected to have grown by 16% in its fiscal first quarter, which ended in December. (The sole blip, in the previous quarter, was caused by a shortage of micro-processors for Apple's hottest new computer, the G4.) Profits doubled in the last fiscal year. Best of all, Apple's stock set an all-time high of $118 in early December and has been hovering around $100 ever since, eight times the price at its nadir, shortly after Jobs took over.

Those are pretty good numbers, especially considering that in a world dominated by Microsoft Windows PCs, Apple is the size of a fly. Despite the iMac's runaway success, the company still hasn't managed to push its worldwide market share—close to 10% in the late '80s—much beyond 3%. In fact, its buckets of profits seem to buttress Jobs' belief that the PC industry has grown big and varied enough to accommodate a niche for a high-end BMW-like computer maker. Nor does market share seem to matter one whit when it comes to Apple's ability to alter the course of the PC business—and that, of course, is what gives Steve his biggest buzz.

"I don't want to toot our own horn too much, because it sounds arrogant, but the rest of the industry is trying to copy our every move again, just like in the '80s," says Jobs. "Every PC manufacturer is trying to copy the iMac in one way or another. And you can bet they'll be cloning iBook next year. The same goes for our software. Our QuickTime streaming video player has this sleek, brushed-metal look on the screen, and our iMovie digital video editing software on the new iMacs lets you make your home movies actually viewable. Well, a month ago Bill Gates announced that Microsoft's next Windows multimedia player was going to feature a brushed-metal interface, and that they're coming out with Windows Movie Maker. So now we've got Microsoft copying us again too. And I don't mind. I don't mind."

Microsoft, for its part, couldn't be happier about Apple's resurgence. For one thing, its business selling Macintosh applications software is hugely profitable. And its lawyers, now in the throes of trying to settle Microsoft's celebrated federal antitrust case, can point to Apple's comeback as hard evidence that the PC industry does foster at least a little competition. Best of all, the controversial $150 million investment Microsoft made in Apple after Jobs came back in 1997—which seemed a charity donation at the time—now looks downright prescient.

So we can forgive Jobs if he gloats a little. Things are clicking in both his CEO gigs. Pixar's *Toy Story 2* was the holiday season's biggest box-office hit. As for Apple, Job says, "It has been a bigger company, but it has never been more capable or more profitable than today. The best thing is that we're done patching the place up. Now we're marching forward on all fronts." No wonder he used the Macworld forum to announce that he has dropped the "interim" from his CEO title. This guy clearly plans to stick around. (For more on Jobs' thoughts, feelings, and plans for Apple and his future, including an explanation of why he still won't let the company pay him more than $1 a year, see the interview that follows this story.)

AS MUCH AS JOBS LOVES to develop gee-whiz hardware, system software has always been what really distinguishes the Macintosh. At Jobs' insistence, the Mac was the first PC to popularize the now-familiar graphical user interface, or GUI, in which you use a mouse, onscreen windows, and icons to operate the computer. Microsoft and Sun Microsystems have openly copied many of Apple's interface innovations in their Windows and Solaris operating systems.

Apple added more and more capabilities to the Mac OS over the years to make it more robust. But the company never tinkered much with the interface. That has changed with Mac OS X, a top-to-bottom rewrite of the operating system. Mac users will see differences on their screens as soon as they load OS X and its new user interface, Aqua. The software, which all recent Macs and iMacs will be able to use, continues to employ windows, icons, pull-down menus, buttons, and dialogue boxes, but they've been subtly transformed. As with iMac hardware, translucence is a key design element—you can peer through command boxes, for instance, to glimpse the documents underneath. The interface introduces something called a dock—a band of animated icons and miniaturized windows along the bottom of the screen. Designed to cut clutter, they streamline humdrum tasks like clicking from program to program and document to document. The interface aims to be "better yet familiar," says Avie Tevanian, senior vice president for software engineering, Jobs' former chief soul mate at Next and his present one at Apple. "Aqua pushes the envelope, but it doesn't create a whole new envelope, because we wanted to preserve the best elements of the Mac OS."

The truly radical changes in OS X are under the hood. Based on Next's operating system, OS X is actually a blood relative of industrial-strength Unix operating systems like Sun's Solaris and Linux, the current freeware sensation; hence OS X is far less likely to crash than any previous Mac OS. Because of its lineage, Mac OS X may not even require a Mac; with a little fiddling by Apple, it could be made to work in Dells, Compaqs, or other Intel-based PCs. (Tevanian stresses that this is not one of Apple's immediate priorities.)

OS X handles onscreen graphics in a unique way that allows a Mac to display just about any kind of document the user might receive over the Internet, even if he doesn't have the program used to create it. Though it is fundamentally different from earlier Mac operating systems, it boasts a mode that will enable it to run most existing Mac programs (Jobs calls these classic applications) almost as smoothly as they run on today's iMacs.

The most profound advantages of OS X will reveal themselves as developers craft new software for it. There will be two ways to do that. "We've made it easy for developers to recompile their older applications so that they can run 'native' in the new operating system with much better perfor-

OLIVER LAUDE

APPLE SOFTWARE SAGE AVIE TEVANIAN

mance and stability," explains Tevanian. "We're also providing a whole set of development tools and interfaces we call Cocoa that lets programmers build brand-new programs in about a tenth the time it would take to write them for any other operating system." Tevanian hopes Cocoa will tempt developers—who deserted by the hundreds in recent years as Apple's market share waned—to start building Mac applications again.

Jobs, as usual, has a vivid metaphor ready to explain why Apple geeks will be able to improve OS X faster than Microsoft geeks can improve Windows: "Think of Windows and our older Mac OS's as houses built with two-by-fours. You can build that kind of house only so high before it collapses from its own weight. So as you start to build it higher, you have to spend 90% of your time going back down to shore up the lower floors with more two-by-fours before you can go on to build the next floor. That leaves you with only 10% of your engineering budget to spend on actually innovating—it's why new versions of Windows always come out way late. On the other hand, OS X is like a software space frame made out of titanium. It is so strong and light and well designed that it lets us spend all of our resources innovating, not reinforcing the foundations."

AS SOPHISTICATED as it is underneath, OS X is intended first and foremost for consumers, using state-of-the-art programming to enhance and simplify the computing experience. "Who says consumers don't want and need the best technology?" says Phil Schiller, Apple's vice president for worldwide marketing. "Always before, the consumer market was considered the tail of the dog. Well, we're driving advanced technology back to the consumer. That's how the whole PC business started."

Jobs' passions have always been cool hardware and mouthwatering system software. But lately he is just as smitten by the Internet's potential to add a special dimension to the Macintosh user experience. "I actually think that our new Internet services are going to be the equal of OS X in making the Macintosh stand out," he says. "They are so hot."

Of the free iTools he unveiled in San Francisco, some are improved versions of services you can find elsewhere on the web; a couple are truly novel. All are designed to take particular advantage of Macs equipped with OS 9, Apple's current operating system, and OS X when it hits the market. Says Eddie Cue, senior director of Internet services: "We're the first to really let the operating system play a key part in Internet computing. In some cases you won't even need your browser to take advantage of an iTool." Here's a quick rundown of Apple's first batch of iTools:

iDisk: Probably the most intriguing new Apple service,

iDisk provides every Mac user with 20 megabytes of free data-storage space on the company's servers (if you want more you'll have to pay for it). That gives the user a place to build online archives of digital photos, documents, and even digital film clips. iDisk also provides a "public folder" so that you can make stuff available for other web surfers to see or download. Other Internet services offer free storage, but what makes iDisk unique is that, on the user's computer screen, it looks and behaves just like a disk drive inside the machine. All the user has to do is drag and drop files onto the iDisk icon, and the next time the Mac goes online, it automatically uploads the data to Apple's servers. The iDisk is key to several other iTools.

HomePage: Websites like Homestead.com and Yahoo's GeoCities offer free homepages, but Apple promises that Mac owners will get their personal website up and running much more quickly and easily if they go to apple.com. Apple will provide templates and plug-in features like guest books and visitor counters; anyone with an iDisk will be able to easily and instantly update his site with digital photos, sound bites, documents, or video clips.

KidSafe: Many parents worry about X-rated, violent, or otherwise objectionable stuff their kids might come across while surfing what often seems the Wild Wild Web. Apple's solution is radically different from conventional kid-protection software, which tries to filter out what kids shouldn't see on the fly. By contrast, KidSafe, which is controlled directly by the Mac OS, specifies what sites kids can see. To accomplish this, Apple assembled an advisory board of teachers and librarians to certify that specific websites are "KidSafe." The board has already approved 50,000 sites; the goal is to add 10,000 each month. Parents also may add to their children's list of permissible destinations. Because KidSafe works in the operating system and not the browser, kids can't easily turn it off or get around it.

THERE ARE OTHER ITOOLS. Mac.com is a free e-mail service that can be used with any e-mail application or Internet browser; iCards is a free e-mail greeting-card service. Apple has also cooked up an Internet wayfinder called iReview. Unlike conventional search engines and portals, iReview offers quality ratings for

MICHAEL SEXTON

thousands of websites in a dozen or so categories, making it easier to figure out which are really worth visiting. The service provides two kinds of ratings: It employs a panel of web experts to review and rank sites. (Any Internet surfer can look at them.) And if you are a Mac user, iReview also invites you to weigh in with your own opinion and keeps a running score for each site. And like all the iTool sites, iReview has a quality that reflects Apple's counterculture roots: It won't accept advertising. Apple's own branding on the sites is discreet—usually a small Apple logo at the top of each web page.

Offering services exclusively for Mac users raises the possibility that Apple may start a dangerous trend: breaking up the Internet into exclusive, jealously guarded preserves. Jobs insists that can't happen: "The Internet has resisted all efforts to Balkanize it. The point is that iMac users can get everything else on the web that everyone else gets, plus all these new services." You may buy that or not, but there is no question that computing's No. 1 impresario is on a roll. Talk to him a little longer and it becomes clear that while Jobs has lots he's proud of—Apple's new OS X and Internet strategy, its colorful hardware, its financial turnaround—what really gets him cranked is the buff condition of Apple itself.

It's true: Jobs has marshaled the management team, the operational prowess, and the engineering skill that enable Apple to dream up and deliver genuinely innovative products and services quickly. Long known for its melodramatic, snafu-ridden, often downright dysfunctional culture, the company now routinely meets and even beats deadlines. Most of the surprises it springs on customers and investors are of the positive kind.

That's the real reason Jobs stripped the word "interim" from his title. "I took a walk with my wife the other night and was telling her how, the way I see it, Apple offers me a base that I would be foolish to walk away from," he says. "Think about it. By the end of this year we'll have maybe $5 billion in the bank, the Macintosh will be thriving, hopefully our Internet services will be a big hit, and our engineering teams will be operating at the peak of their games. I'm always keeping my eyes open for the next big opportunity, but the way the world is now, it will take enormous resources, both in money and in engineering talent, to make it happen. I don't know what that next big thing might be, but I have a few ideas. Whatever it is, it will be much easier and better to use Apple as the springboard than to have to start from scratch." During that same walk, he told his wife he plans to stay with Apple at least four or five more years. In Internet time, that would be forever.

MICHAEL O'NEILL

APPLE'S $1-A-YEAR MAN

NOW THAT STEVE JOBS has showed his hand on Apple's Internet and system software strategies and dropped the "interim" from his title, other questions loom. He's always denied it, but isn't it true that his old company, Next, did wind up taking over Apple? Will there ever be an encore to the 15-year-old Macintosh? Short of that, does Apple have any plans to jump into the "Internet appliance" fray? Will Apple ever build computers for businesspeople again? And what, pray tell, does Steve think of all these young Internet zillionaires? Let's ask.

Practically every technology that your old company, Next, possessed when Apple acquired it in 1997 is now being used by Apple in some strategic way. This must seem like sweet vindication.

The thing about Next was that we produced something that was truly brilliant for an audience that our heart really wasn't into selling to—namely, the enterprise.

I suppose if you were writing a book, this would be a great plot line, because the whole thing circles back. All of a sudden, it's coming out for the market that we would've liked to create it for in the first place—i.e., consumers. So it's a good ending.

So now you're at the beginning of something else. How did Apple's Internet services come together? It seems like it happened quickly.

We entered 1999 with a feeling of having had tremendous success in 1998, what with the introduction of the iMac and all. And I was getting suggestions from people inside and outside Apple that we needed to think about starting an ISP [Internet service provider] business, just like Compaq and Gateway and Dell.

I was dragging my feet because it just didn't feel right. The more I thought about it, the more I saw that you can separate services from Internet access, and use those unique services to create incredible competitive differentiation, regardless of who provides the access. We didn't have to be an access provider ourselves to get most of the benefits.

Remember, we have a lot of market power in that we own an extremely popular Internet-access device. If you look at most ISPs, their No. 1 expense by a mile is customer acquisition. Well, we're acquiring new customers all the time; one third of all iMac customers are first-time computer owners. We can help those hundreds of thousands of newbies—who also happen to have incredible demographics—find an ISP. So we've made Earthlink our exclusive ISP; we'll get paid a bounty and they'll get new customers.

I'd say the big light bulb on services came on about nine months ago. The big light bulb being: "Wait a minute. We own a major operating system. Why don't we build some services that work uniquely with it to give us unfair competitive advantage?" Everything fell into place this fall. Our secret weapon to be able to build these services so quickly is OS X and the set of programmers' development tools that goes with it, WebObjects. We really do eat our own dog food around here.

Given that you're emphasizing Mac OS X and iTools, and not even introducing new hardware at a time of year when you customarily do, should Apple's new slogan be something like "It's the software, stupid"?

We're still heavily into the box. We love the box. We have amazing computers today, and amazing hardware in the pipeline. I still spend a lot of my time working on new computers, and it will always be a primal thing for Apple. But the user experience is what we care about most, and we're expanding that experience beyond the box by making better use of the Internet. The user experience now entails four things: the hardware, the operating system, the applications, and the Net. We want to do all four uniquely well for our customers.

You seem more focused than ever on the consumer market. Why do you think it holds so much promise?

A lot of people can't get past the fact that we're not going after the enterprise market. But that's like saying, "How can the Gap be successful not making suits?" Well, we don't make wingtips here either.

Then again, big companies are beginning to buy a lot from us simply because they like our jellybeans. If you want to have your employee up and on your intranet in seven minutes and if you want to have lower maintenance costs than you would running Windows, iMacs are great. But we make zero effort to sell to big companies.

We think that a lot more big businesses will eventually come back to us, because *Fortune* 500 companies use a lot of consumer products. If you want a minivan for your

MICHAEL O'NEILL

corporation, you don't have one custom made; you go to the Chrysler dealer and buy one. They make great minivans, even though they don't make them for corporate America. Even so, a lot of big companies—including ours—buy them.

It's really hard to serve multiple masters—different sets of customers with completely different points of view, requirements, and ways of approaching computing. I think Microsoft is experiencing this.

I've always believed that the biggest market for PCs is consumers. The Mac was originally intended to be a consumer PC. One of the big arguments I had with [former Apple CEO] John Sculley was that the Mac was designed to sell for $1,000. Yes, we overshot a little, and it cost too much to make to sell for that, but even so, I thought it should have sold for between $1,500 and $1,799. John wanted to bump it up to $2,499. His vision was to keep on going all the way up and have Macs selling for $5,000 or $10,000. After I left, that's exactly what Apple did.

By some measures, it worked. Apple made a fortune, although not as much as we're making today. What they didn't understand was that they had thrown away one of the greatest chances they'd ever get to win market share. They went for $1 billion in extra profits over four or five years when what they really should have done was tell everybody they would make "normal" profits and go for market share.

Just about every other computer maker is exploring new digital devices that can tap into the Internet, but you're still focused on personal computers. Why?

Everyone's talking about "information appliances" and other "post-PC" devices. So far, there have only been two or three that have succeeded—the Palm and game machines like the Sony PlayStation and possibly the cellphone. None of the others have succeeded. Why is that?

Well, if you look at the Internet, you can see it is absolutely optimized for PCs. All the pages are laid out to be viewed on a PC. That's one reason WebTV—a device that displays websites on a normal TV—has failed. Beyond that, the web is rich with things like Java and QuickTime and RealPlayer and MP3 sound files. By the time you build a device that [can handle those things], you've got something that is like a PC without the disk drives and is only about $50 cheaper than a PC or an iMac.

Then you ask your user if they care about storing anything. Do you care about storing MP3 files, or would you rather wait a few minutes to download them every time you want to hear them? Do you care about storing the photos you take with your digital camera? The answer is almost al-

ways yes. It's not that expensive to add a disk drive to let you do these things, and once you do, you're back to a PC. The only way to make it any cheaper is to start giving up things.

Apple is very much weighted toward the consumer electronics space right now, because we're selling to a lot of consumers and we want to help them get more benefits from hooking up various things to computers and to each other. The perfect example is the digital camcorder and the iMac. It's amazing what you can do when you plug these things together—we call it iMovies.

I won't lie, we're working on other digital devices like everybody else. But I'm not convinced that customers won't pay a little bit more for a device that's not going to be obsolete in a year and that's going to give them the full Internet experience, not an "Internet Jr." experience.

What has always distinguished the products of the companies you've led is the design aesthetic. Is your obsession with design an inborn instinct or what?

We don't have good language to talk about this kind of thing. In most people's vocabularies, design means veneer. It's interior decorating. It's the fabric of the curtains and the sofa. But to me, nothing could be further from the meaning of design. Design is the fundamental soul of a man-made creation that ends up expressing itself in successive outer layers of the product or service. The iMac is not just the color or translucence or the shape of the shell. The essence of the iMac is to be the finest possible consumer computer in which each element plays together.

On our latest iMac, I was adamant that we get rid of the fan, because it is much more pleasant to work on a computer that doesn't drone all the time. That was not just "Steve's decision" to pull out the fan; it required an enormous engineering effort to figure out how to manage power better and do a better job of thermal conduction through the machine. That is the furthest thing from veneer. It was at the core of the product the day we started.

This is what customers pay us for—to sweat all these details so it's easy and pleasant for them to use our computers. We're supposed to be really good at this. That doesn't mean we don't listen to customers, but it's hard for them to tell you what they want when they've never seen anything remotely like it. Take desktop video editing. I never got one request from someone who wanted to edit movies on his computer. Yet now that people see it, they say, "Oh my God, that's great!"

I don't see enough innovation like that in our industry. My position coming back to Apple was that our industry was in a coma. It reminded me of Detroit in the '70s, when American cars were boats on wheels. That's why we have a really good chance to be a serious player again.

You and Apple have been responsible for popularizing the personal computer. What will be the next big breakthrough?
People are always asking, "What will be the next Macintosh?" My answer still is, "I don't know and I don't care." Everybody at Apple has been working really hard the last two and a half years to reinvent this company. We've made tremendous progress. My goal has been to get Apple healthy enough so that if we do figure out the next big thing, we can seize the moment. Getting a company healthy doesn't happen overnight. You have to rebuild some organizations, clean up others that don't make sense, and build up new engineering capabilities.

Another priority was to make Apple more entrepreneurial and startup-like. So we immediately reorganized, drastically narrowed the product line, and changed compensation for senior managers so they get a lot of stock but no cash bonuses. The upshot is that the place feels more like a young company.

We're trying to use the swiftness and creativity in a younger-style company, and yet bring to bear the tremendous resources of a company the size of Apple to do large projects that you could never handle at a startup. A startup could never do the new iMac. Literally 2,000 people worked on it. A startup could never do Mac OS X. It's not easy at a big company either, but Apple now has the management and systems in place to get things like that done. I can't emphasize how rare that is. That's what makes Sony and Disney so special.

Now when we see new things or opportunities, we can seize them. In fact, we have already seized a few, like desktop movies, wireless networking, and iTools. A creative period like this lasts only maybe a decade, but it can be a golden decade if we manage it properly.

You've finally done away with the word "interim" in your title. But you still only let Apple pay you $1 a year. Why don't you take any salary or stock yet?
The board has made several incredibly generous offers. I have turned them all down for a few reasons. For the first year I did not want the shareholders and employees of Pixar to think their CEO was going on a camping trip over to Apple never to return. After two and a half years, I think that the management teams at Pixar and at Apple have

demonstrated that we can handle this situation. That's why I dropped the "interim" from my title. I'm still called iCEO, though, because I think it's cool.

Bottom line is, I didn't return to Apple to make a fortune. I've been very lucky in my life and already have one. When I was 25, my net worth was $100 million or so. I decided then that I wasn't going to let it ruin my life. There's no way you could ever spend it all, and I don't view wealth as something that validates my intelligence. I just wanted to see if we could work together to turn this thing around when the company was literally on the verge of bankruptcy. The decision to go without pay has served me well.

Do you ever look around and think that a younger generation is driving this industry now?
I had dinner in Seattle at Bill Gates' house a couple of weeks ago. We were both remarking how at one time we were the youngest guys in this business, and now we're the graybeards.

When I got started, I was 20 or 21, and my role models were the semiconductor guys like Robert Noyce and Andy Grove of Intel, and of course Bill Hewlett and David Packard. They were out not so much to make money as to change the world and to build companies that could keep growing and changing. They left incredible legacies.

It's hard to tell with these Internet startups if they're really interested in building companies or if they're just interested in the money. I can tell you, though: If they don't really want to build a company, they won't luck into it. That's because it's so hard that if you don't have a passion, you'll give up. There were times in the first two years when we could have given up and sold Apple, and it probably would've died.

But then, the rewarding thing isn't merely to start a company or to take it public. It's like when you're a parent. Although the birth experience is a miracle, what's truly rewarding is living with your child and helping him grow up.

The problem with the Internet startup craze isn't that too many people are starting companies; it's that too many people aren't sticking with it. That's somewhat understandable, because there are many moments that are filled with despair and agony, when you have to fire people and cancel things and deal with very difficult situations. That's when you find out who you are and what your values are.

So when these people sell out, even though they get fabulously rich, they're gypping themselves out of one of the potentially most rewarding experiences of their unfolding lives. Without it, they may never know their values or how to keep their newfound wealth in perspective.

FOUR PEOPLE WHO RARELY SPEAK PUBLICLY ABOUT JOBS EXPLAIN WHAT MAKES HIM ONE OF THE BEST BUSINESS MINDS OF ALL TIME.

Andy Grove
Former chairman and CEO,
Intel

WHEN YOU TALK ABOUT STEVE, you need to distinguish between Jobs 1, the young man who started Apple, and Jobs 2, the guy who came back to Apple and turned it around. During the Jobs 1 era, some of us from Silicon Valley were invited to a dinner in Palo Alto. It was 1983. At one point during the meal, Steve stands up and yells, "Nobody over 30 can possibly understand what computing is all about."

I pulled him aside, waved my finger, and lectured him, telling him, "You're incredibly arrogant. You don't know what you don't know." His response was, "Teach me. Tell me what I should know." We had lunch and talked, mostly about personal stuff. I don't think I taught him anything. But he was wrong when he singled a generation out. How old was Steve when the iPod came out—46?

As Jobs 2 he became the turnaround artist of the decade. There's no other company in technology that's started with a strong core business and developed another very strong one. The rest of us are lucky, or good, [if we're] right once.
—*Interview by Michael V. Copeland*

Andrea Jung
Chairman and CEO,
Avon

ALL OF US LIKE TO THINK THAT we're as focused on the consumer and the end-user experience as Steve is—that maniacal passion for the best phone, the best MP3 player, the best PC, the best retail experience. He does it in a very black-and-white way, while the rest of the world gets caught up in the gray—or caught up in themselves. He makes it sound so simple, but he's taking on things that are extraordinarily complex and arguably risky. He's laser-focused on getting it right. It's a great lesson in this quarter-to-quarter world. With seven directors, the Apple board—which I am on—is smaller than most, including Avon's. There's an extraordinary openness in the boardroom. Any board member would feel free to challenge an idea or raise a concern. It's not only been gratifying, it's been great. I feel like I'm part of history being made. I leave Apple board meetings thinking, "I've got to do a better job."
—*Interview by Patricia Sellers*

Larry Ellison
Co-Founder and CEO,
Oracle

I REMEMBER WHEN STEVE was my neighbor in Woodside, Calif., and he had no furniture. It struck me that there wasn't furniture good enough for Steve in the world. He'd rather have nothing if he couldn't have perfection. And I jokingly said, "The difference between me and Steve is that I'm willing to live with the best the world can provide. With Steve that's not always good enough." And if you look at how he tackles building a phone, or building a laptop, he really is in pursuit of this technical and aesthetic perfection. And he just won't compromise.

But he's never been motivated by money. Once we were hiking, and Steve looked at me, put his right hand on my left shoulder and his left hand on my right shoulder, and said, "Larry, that's why it's really important that I'm your friend. See, you don't need any more money."

He's enormously proud of the fact that Apple is now the highest-valued company in Silicon Valley, higher than Cisco, higher than Intel, higher than Google, higher than Oracle.
—*Interview by Adam Lashinsky*

Marc Andreessen
General partner,
Andreessen Horowitz

I DON'T KNOW if publicly this is known, but when he came back [to Apple in 1997], they were weeks away from going bankrupt. He went from weeks away from bankruptcy to building these kinds of products. He was under pressure the entire time. But he set the performance standard for product thinking and product execution that all the rest of us should aspire to hit. [And he's taught us that] in this industry, the products really, really matter.
—*Interview by Adam Lashinsky*

FROM LEFT: BEN BAKER—REDUX; RAY TAMARRA; JUSTIN SULLIVAN—GETTY; ROBYN TWOMEY

 **The Legacy of Steve Jobs**

 **Chapter Three**

 **Fortune**
November 12, 2001

COURTESY APPLE

APPLE'S 21ST-CENTURY WALKMAN

CEO STEVE JOBS THINKS HE HAS SOMETHING PRETTY NIFTY. AND IF HE'S RIGHT, HE MIGHT EVEN SPOOK SONY AND MATSUSHITA. BY BRENT SCHLENDER

"**W**E BUILD THE WHOLE WIDGET.**" That's one of Steve Jobs' favorite explanations for why he thinks Apple Computer's products are so darn cool. What he means is that Apple's own engineers design much of the hardware and virtually all the key software for Macintosh computers, rather than merely wielding screwdrivers to assemble prefabricated kits cooked up by the geeks at Intel and Microsoft. The result is a distinctive line of computers that are more stylish and reliable and easy to use than their Wintel PC counterparts, and that, despite Apple's Lilliputian 5% market share, often set the aesthetic and technical standards for what a PC should be. Several of Apple's Macs have even wound up at New York City's Museum of Modern Art as examples of exceptional design and engineering. But "widgets" they are not.

Now, with the introduction of the sleek little iPod, a $399 personal digital-music player, Steve has finally built a widget. About the size of a pack of cigarettes, the iPod is more than just a portable sound machine, however. It's a new kind of gadget that has the potential to change how we think about personal audio-entertainment gizmos, much as Sony's first pocket-size transistor radio did in 1958, and the Sony Walkman portable stereo tape player did 20 years later. The progeny of an eight-month crash-development project, the iPod also vividly illustrates how Apple's engineering and software skills could make it a force to be reckoned with in the consumer electronics business long dominated by leviathans like Sony and Matsushita. "This is the 21st-century Walkman," boasts Jobs, as he lovingly fondles an iPod.

If you took a ball-peen hammer to the hermetically sealed stainless-steel and polycarbonate case, the components you'd find inside the iPod wouldn't seem all that extraordinary, at least by computer-industry standards. There's a teensy five-gigabyte hard drive, capacious enough to store up to 100 hours of MP3 music files—the equivalent of about 100 CDs. There's a lithium-polymer battery that can power the iPod for ten hours between full charges. The box also contains 32 megabytes' worth of memory chips—far more than a typical Palm organizer—and an array of other circuitry, including a microprocessor like those used in handhelds. And it sports a high-resolution liquid-crystal display about the size of a matchbook.

The most unusual component is an ingenious two-inch-diameter thumb-wheel on the faceplate for scrolling through hierarchical menus on the six-line display. (I mastered the scroll-wheel interface in a couple of minutes. It's easiest to use with one hand.) Aside from the standard headphone jack, there's only one other socket, for connecting the iPod to a computer via a special Firewire cable, which not only allows high-speed transfers of digital files but also recharges the iPod's battery at the same time.

"So what?" you say. Most of those components and features show up in other digital devices, from Pocket PCs to laptops, and besides, portable MP3 players that link up to computers have been around for several years. The big differences, however, are the high-speed connection and the software that makes it all go. When you plug the Firewire cable into a Macintosh (a PC-compatible version won't come out till next summer at the earliest), the Mac immediately recognizes the iPod and starts up the iTunes music-management program included with all Apple computers. If you don't have the latest version of iTunes, no problem. The iPod has it right on its little disk, and it will zap the software directly to your Mac. iTunes keeps track of MP3 music files that have either been downloaded from the Internet or "ripped" from a conventional audio CD. It also lets users set up playlists of favorite songs and sort them by artist, album, or title. Within seconds, the Mac automatically starts to transfer all the music and playlists to the iPod. Downloading 1,000 songs takes only about 10 minutes. And the next time you connect, iTunes quickly transfers only new music and playlists, much like "syncing" a Palm or a Pocket PC. As Jobs puts it, "Plug it in. Whirrrrrr. Done."

That is what Steve really means when he talks about "building the whole widget." Until the iPod came along, most MP3 players were awkward afterthoughts that only a propeller-head could love. They had much slower USB connections for downloading music from a PC. A single CD's worth of MP3s would take three to five minutes to transfer over USB, vs. five to 10 seconds for the iPod. Nor did previous MP3 players have the smarts to accommodate multiple playlists that you put together on your computer, or a versatile user interface for navigating quickly through hundreds of titles. But then, it didn't much matter, because most players could store only a couple of dozen songs. A few other MP3 players on the market do hold as much as the iPod, but they're much bulkier, and finding the songs you want to hear on them is as annoying as setting the digital clock on your VCR.

BRENT SCHLENDER

WHY IN THE WORLD would Apple want to jump from the frying pan of the virtually profitless PC industry into the roaring fire of the hypercompetitive consumer electronics business? After all, just a few days before Apple's splashy introduction of the iPod, Intel announced that it would close down its own disappointing consumer electronics division, which made, among other things, portable MP3 players, digital still cameras, kiddie videocameras, and a much ballyhooed digital microscope.

For starters, the iPod fits right into Jobs' so-called Digital Hub strategy for the Macintosh. In the past 18 months Apple has introduced several free "digital lifestyle" software applications that let Macintosh computers hook up to various genres of consumer electronics products so that users can play around with the digital content they create. There's iMovie for editing home videos made with camcorders, and iDVD for burning those edited movies onto a DVD. And, of course, there's iTunes, which, besides managing and playing back MP3 audio files on a Mac, can also burn them onto conventional audio CDs. In the next few months Apple will probably release another application for managing digital photos.

Jobs hopes those "iApps" will stir consumers to buy more Macs, but he recognizes that the strategy could also drive sales of digital gadgetry, and he wants a piece of that action. Camcorders and digital still cameras are beyond

Apple's ken, but digital-music players are remarkably similar to computer peripherals. (The iPod, when you think about it, is basically a portable hard drive.) And, better yet, judging from the hundreds of millions of Walkman-type products in use, portable music devices have almost universal appeal.

Moreover, electronics industry analysts believe that the iPod may yield more profit per unit than Apple's slick iBook laptop computers, which cost three times as much, mainly because so much less goes into it. The iPods hit store shelves Nov. 10. Jobs won't say how many Apple hopes to sell, other than to say "as many as we can make." When pushed, he concedes that contract manufacturers in Taiwan have tooled up to pound out "hundreds of thousands a quarter," which would translate into hundreds of millions of dollars in new revenues in 2002. Such sums aren't chicken feed for a company that saw its annual sales erode in fiscal 2001 by 33%, to $5.4 billion. Only a week before the iPod's unveiling, Apple reported that fiscal fourth-quarter profits declined from $170 million last year to $66 million (most of which was investment income from its $4 billion cash hoard). Now the company hopes to see a material gain in profits in the December quarter, thanks to the little guy—if it sells as well as Steve thinks it will.

The project to develop the iPod came as close to instant gratification as the computer industry ever gets. It was only last April that Jobs asked Jon Rubinstein, the senior vice president for hardware development, to put together a SWAT team that could produce a device in time for the Christmas shopping season. Says Rubinstein: "Senior management had been talking about something like the iPod since late last year, but we started with a clean sheet of paper." Even by Apple's tightlipped standards, secrecy was intense. Rubinstein quickly recruited a handful of hardware and software engineers, including several from outside the company, without telling any of them exactly what they'd be working on until they signed up. Other Apple engineers drifted in and out of the project as their expertise was needed, and some were never told the purpose of their efforts either. At any one time, about 50 people were working on the iPod.

The engineering team confronted a host of thorny problems, not least of which was figuring out how to cut power consumption so that users wouldn't have to worry all the time about running out of juice. In essence, the iPod loads songs onto its memory chips so that the power-hogging hard drive can shut down during playback; the result is a 10-hour battery life, vs. two or so for other MP3 players.

While the team worked on the innards, Jonathan Ive, Apple's vice president for industrial design, took on the job of creating the look and feel of the device, including the scroll-wheel feature. "Like everyone else on the project, I knocked myself out, not so much because it was a challenge—which it was—but because I wanted to have one," he says. "Only later, as it came together, did the broader significance of what we were working on become apparent."

Indeed, although priority No. 1 was to make the iPod the ultimate personal digital-music player, the team also knew they were designing what was in effect a computer platform that could be improved with software upgrades and adapted to other uses. That's because, like a PC, the iPod has its own operating system, a microprocessor, and lots of memory. In fact, the initial model can double as a portable hard drive for holding computer files of any type—digital photos, documents, or arrays of data.

So you don't have to be a rocket scientist to imagine how Apple might one day build other configurations of the iPod outfitted with, say, a larger full-color screen, or the ability to work with other iApps that manage videoclips and personal calendars. And while Apple never discusses work in progress, the iPod platform might also underpin a whole range of Apple consumer electronics devices, like a home content server or even an enhanced cellphone, each of which would link back to a Mac in some way.

At first glance, the idea of equating the iPod to such seminal products as Sony's transistor radio and Walkman seems like typical Jobsian hyperbole. At the very least, the iPod will have a tough time matching the Walkman's mass appeal. Apple will have to develop a version of iTunes for non-Macintosh computers or "sync" with at least one maker of jukebox software already popular on those machines. Owners of most Wintel PCs will also need to add a Firewire connection at a cost of $100 to $150—just the sort of nuisance and expense that can slow a technological revolution. And while the $399 iPod delivers far more bang for the buck than the $249 Rio MP3 player (which holds only two hours of music), it still costs 10 times more than a Walkman or its many copycats.

Even so, Jobs may have a point in invoking the Walkman. That product, because it employed cassette tapes as the medium for recording music, marked the beginning of the marginalization of the analog LP record and brought big changes to the recording industry. If music lovers didn't buy prerecorded cassettes to play on their portable players, they simply dubbed their LPs onto tape and put

HARDWARE CHIEF JON RUBINSTEIN [LEFT] AND LEAD DESIGNER JONATHAN IVE BROUGHT THE iPOD TO LIFE IN JUST EIGHT MONTHS.

THOMAS BROENIG

over the Internet. Hence the celebrated Napster legal donnybrook, in which record companies persuaded the courts to crack down on websites that facilitated digital song swapping. But MP3 technology, because it allows so much music to be electronically stored in such a relatively compact space, has triggered other changes in how people use the recorded music they legally own—changes that could encourage record companies to alter yet again how they package and distribute their music. And the iPod may hasten this change.

That's because Apple, a staunch defender of its own intellectual property, took great care to make it difficult for anyone to use the iPod to share recorded music. While the device can automatically download digital music from your own Mac, Apple made it a tricky proposition to transfer music from your iPod to a different computer; you can't easily use your iPod to collect music from someone else's computer either. Steve explains how it works: "If you try to sync your iPod with someone else's Mac, it stops you and gives you a choice—either you can cancel the request to sync to this 'foreign' Mac and unplug your iPod, or you can agree to let it blow away all the music you now have on your iPod before it downloads the music library from the new sync partner. But then, when you go back to your own Mac, the same thing happens."

Besides, says Jobs, the whole point of the iPod isn't to help you share music with your friends; it's to let you carry around your entire personal music collection wherever you go. So, like the Walkman before it, the iPod, if it really catches on, could change the format in which music lovers "consume" much of their music. Most will still buy their music, which will keep the record companies and recording artists happy. But after ripping their CDs into MP3s and loading them onto the iPod, they'll leave the disks on the shelf in their cases for months at a time. That'll even be true for people who want to listen only at home. The iPod can plug into standard audio equipment and bring playlist convenience to the living room; audiophiles unhappy with MP3 sound quality can set the iPod to allot more digital bits to each second of music.

And because Apple has made it so difficult to pirate music with an iPod, maybe, just maybe, the record companies will get brave enough to start selling MP3-format music online bigtime. So, strange as it may seem, if Steve's iPod really does become the Walkman of the 21st century and millions of people pack them in their pockets and purses, the record companies might ultimately be among this widget's biggest fans.

the fragile and unwieldy vinyl disks back on the shelf to gather dust. In other words, LPs became, for the most part, archives, and were soon rendered virtually obsolete by the arrival of the CD digital format in the 1980s.

It was the emergence of MP3 digital-audio compression technology in the late 1990s that really roiled the recording industry and gave musicians apoplexy over the potential for rampant illegal copying and sharing of digital music

Chapter Four

THE "i" YEARS

Steve Jobs was one of the first to see the vast business potential of the Internet. With the launch of iTunes in 2001, he started creating businesses that merged consumer products with the web, which eventually led to everything from the iPhone to the iCloud. It was during these years that Jobs also launched what was to become one of the most successful retail projects in history: the Apple Store. However, he was not without his tribulations. Jobs was diagnosed with cancer and later embroiled in a stock options scandal.

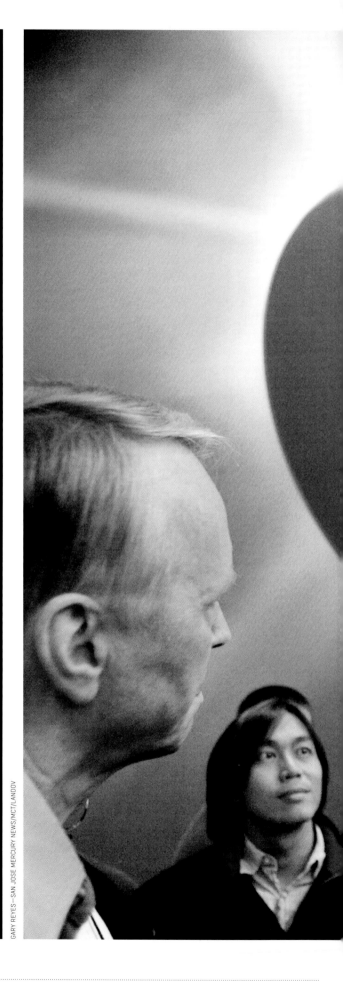

GARY REYES—SAN JOSE MERCURY NEWS/MCT/LANDOV

THE LAUNCH OF THE iPHONE IN 2007 AT MACWORLD IN SAN FRANCISCO

SONGS IN THE KEY OF STEVE

STEVE JOBS MAY HAVE JUST CREATED THE FIRST GREAT LEGAL ONLINE MUSIC SERVICE THAT'S GOT THE RECORD BIZ SINGING HIS PRAISES.

BY DEVIN LEONARD

STEVE JOBS LOVES MUSIC. But as with a lot of geeks in Silicon Valley, his musical tastes are a little retro. He worships Bob Dylan and is the kind of obsessive Beatles fan who can talk your ear off about why Ringo is an underappreciated drummer. So Dr. Dre, the rap-music Midas whose protégés include Snoop Dogg and Eminem, is the last person you'd expect to see huddled with Jobs, for hours on end, at Apple headquarters in Cupertino, Calif. No, they weren't discussing whether John or Paul was the more talented Beatle. Rather, Steve had invited Dr. Dre up from Los Angeles for a private demonstration of Apple's latest product. After checking it out, Dre had this to say: "Man, somebody finally got it right."

The product that wowed him was the iTunes Music Store, a new digital service for Mac users offering songs from all five major music companies—Universal, Warner, EMI, Sony, and BMG. Though Apple had yet to sell a single song by the time *Fortune* went to press, Jobs is already causing a stir in the record business. Forget about rumors that Apple is bidding for Vivendi's Universal Music Group, the world's largest record company. Jobs says he has absolutely no interest in buying a record company.

The real buzz in the music trade is that Steve has just created what is easily the most promising legal digital-music service on the market. "I think it's going to be amazing," says Roger Ames, CEO of the Warner Music Group. Jobs, not surprisingly, is even more effusive. He claims his digital store will forever change not only how music is sold and distributed but also the way artists release and market songs and how they are bought and used by fans.

One thing's for sure: If ever there was an industry in need of transformation, it's the music business. U.S. music sales plunged 8.2% last year, largely because songs are being distributed free on the Internet through illicit file-sharing destinations like KaZaA. Unlike Napster, KaZaA and its brethren have no central servers, making them tougher for the industry to shut down. The majors have tried to come up with legal alternatives. But none of those ventures have taken off because they are too pricey and user-hostile.

The iTunes Music Store, by contrast, is as simple and straightforward as anything Jobs has ever produced. Apple users get to the store by clicking a button on the iTunes 4 jukebox, available for download when the service made its debut on April 28. You can listen to a 30-second preview of any song and then, with one click, buy a high-quality audio copy for 99¢. There's no monthly subscription fee, and consumers have virtually unfettered ownership of the music they download. Jobs is rolling out the iTunes store with previously unreleased material by artists including Bob Dylan, U2, Missy Elliott, and Sheryl Crow. There will be music from bands like the Eagles, who have never before allowed their songs to be sold by a legal digital-music service. And Jobs is personally lobbying other big-name holdouts, like the Rolling Stones and the Beatles, to come aboard.

The iTunes Music Store may be just the thing to get Apple rocking again too. As everyone knows, it's been a tough couple of years for the computer industry as well. Apple swung back into the black in the first quarter of 2003 after two quarterly losses, but its profits were only $14 million, compared with $40 million a year ago. And as popular as Apple's iPod portable MP3 player may be, it contributed less than $25 million of Apple's $1.48 billion in revenues last quarter. So Jobs is betting that by offering customers "Hotel California" for 99¢, he can sell not just more iPods but more Macs too.

Apple's competitors dismiss the iTunes Music Store as a niche product. How, they ask, can Apple have any impact on the music industry when its share of the global computer market is a minuscule 3%? "It's a very positive thing for their community," says Kevin Brangan, a marketing director at SonicBlue, which makes Rio MP3 players. "But their community is a very small percentage of the overall market."

Jobs, however, isn't targeting just Mac users. He plans to roll out a Windows version of iTunes by the end of the year. (Apple already sells a Windows-compatible version of the iPod, which accounts for about half of all units sold.) It is

AMANDA FRIEDMAN

a dramatic departure for Steve, who has deliberately kept the Mac's best features off the screens of the much larger Microsoft-dominated world.

Steve isn't suggesting that his new service will lift the computer industry out of its funk. But he is 100% convinced that the Music Store will rejuvenate the ailing music business. "This will go down in history as a turning point for the music industry," Jobs told *Fortune*. "This is landmark stuff. I can't overestimate it!"

The idea that anybody from Silicon Valley can swoop in and save the music industry seems laughable at first. But by nearly every account, this is not just some Steve Jobs sales job. In fact, the Music Store is being copied by rivals even before it hits the market. The reason, as Dr. Dre noted, is that nobody has come up with a better plan to sell music online. So iTunes or something like it had better work. Otherwise, the music industry as we know it could soon disappear.

T'S A SUNNY AFTERNOON in early April, and Jobs is rhapsodizing about his new music service at Apple headquarters. He is clad in the same outfit he dons nearly every morning so he doesn't have to waste time choosing clothes: a black mock-turtleneck shirt, jeans, and New Balance sneakers. There's been a slight change in his uniform, though. The 48-year-old Apple CEO now rolls up the cuffs of his jeans. (What would Dr. Dre think of that fashion statement?)

But Steve isn't interested in talking about his new look on this day. (He later allowed that he just bought pants that were the wrong size.) He's here to talk music. "It pained us to see the music companies and the technology companies basically threatening to take each other to court and all this other crazy stuff," he explains. "So we thought that rather than sit around and throw stones, we'd actually do something about this."

He was equally appalled by the music industry's reluctance to satisfy the demand for Internet downloading that Napster had unleashed. Who could blame him? After bludgeoning Napster to death in court, record companies promised to launch paid services with the same limitless selection and ease of use.

They did just the opposite. Universal and Sony rolled out a joint venture called Pressplay. AOL Time Warner (the parent of both Warner and *Fortune*'s publisher), Bertelsmann (BMG's owner), EMI, and RealNetworks launched MusicNet. But instead of trying to cooperate to attract customers, the two ventures competed to dominate the digital market. Pressplay wouldn't license its songs to MusicNet,

and MusicNet withheld its tunes from Pressplay.

The result: Neither service had enough songs to attract paying customers, who couldn't care less which record company a particular song comes from. "It was strictly the greed and arrogance of the majors that screwed things up," says Irving Azoff, who manages the Eagles and Christina Aguilera. "They wanted to control every step of the [Internet] distribution process."

The record companies were also fearful about doing anything that might cannibalize CD sales. So they decided to "rent" people music through the Internet. You paid a monthly subscription fee for songs from MusicNet and Pressplay. But you could download MusicNet tunes onto only one computer, and they disappeared if you didn't pay your bill. That may have protected the record companies from piracy, but it didn't do much for consumers. Why fork over $10 a month for a subscription when you can't do anything with your music but listen to it on your PC? Pressplay launched with CD burning but only for a limited number of songs.

At the end of last year, Pressplay and MusicNet licensed their catalogues to each other, ending their standoff. MusicNet also now permits subscribers to burn certain songs onto CDs. But MusicNet users still can't download songs onto portable players. "These devices haven't caught on yet," insists MusicNet CEO Alan McGlade. Never mind that U.S. sales of portable MP3 players soared from 724,000 in 2001 to 1.6 million last year. Pressplay, for its part, lets subscribers download some songs onto devices, but only those that use Microsoft's Windows Media software. That means no iPods.

Pressplay and MusicNet say it's too early for anybody to dismiss them as failures, but it's difficult to see them as anything else. The music industry has little to show for its investment—Sony and Universal are believed to have spent as much as $60 million so far on Pressplay. The two services don't release their subscriber numbers, but Phil Leigh, an analyst at Raymond James, believes that together they have signed up only about 225,000 customers. "It was clear to me in my first 30 days on the job that Pressplay was a first effort and a work-in-progress," says Andrew Lack, who took over as CEO of Sony Music Entertainment in February. "No one was saying, 'This is it. We can't sign up people fast enough.'"

Consequently, the five major record companies have had to slash costs in the face of declining sales. BMG laid off 1,400 people, EMI shed 1,800, and Sony Music recently announced it was reducing headcount by 1,000. Even with those cuts, average profit margins for the five majors have slipped to 5%, compared with 15% to 20% in the late 1980s, when the CD came into vogue. "All the chickens are coming home to roost at the same time," says media analyst Claire Enders. "This industry has never been faced with such cataclysmic conditions before. It has no roadmap on how to cope with them."

The irony is that the music industry has always survived by introducing new formats—from the 78-rpm single to the 33-rpm vinyl LP album in the 1950s, to the cassette tape in the 1970s, to the compact disc, which sparked a re-birth of the industry in the 1980s. Now nearly everyone in the business admits that the only clear path to the future is to come up with a legal online alternative to KaZaA and other illegal file-sharing services. This could be the mother of all format shifts, because it would largely eliminate manufacturing and distribution costs. But nobody in the music industry has been able to get there. "This new technology has swept by us," laments Doug Morris, chairman of the Universal Music Group.

As long as people can get free music online, the music industry's chances of recovery are dim. But stealing songs on the Internet isn't as much fun as it used to be. For one thing, file-sharing services are teeming with viruses. The Recording Industry Association of America has also upped the ante with a new suit accusing four college students of operating piracy networks. That's likely to put a damper on illicit computer activities in many dormitories. In addition, the record companies are planning to introduce new CDs with two sets of the same songs—one that can be played on your CD player and another that you can listen to on your computer but that can't be uploaded onto KaZaA.

In a world where CDs can't be shared on the Internet and music pirates are hauled into court, there may be huge demand for a legitimate digital-music service. But it's going to have to be one that's a lot better than what the music industry has offered so far. Apple's timing, in other words, could hardly have been better.

JOBS DIDN'T SET OUT TO BE the music industry's savior. He was such a latecomer to the digital-music world that some observers wondered if he'd lost his knack for spotting trends long before his competitors. Heck, Apple didn't even include CD burners as standard equipment on its computers until two years ago. But once Jobs focused on music, he was consumed by it. He saw people ripping CD tracks and loading them onto their hard drives. So in 2001 Apple introduced the iTunes

DIGITAL RIVAL: REALNETWORKS CEO GLASER SAYS JOBS IGNORES SOME MUSIC FANS.

jukebox software, which lets users make their own playlists or have the computer select songs randomly.

What else might Mac users wish to do with their MP3 files? Apple engineers were certain they'd want to load them into a pocket-size portable player with a voluminous hard drive. So they created the iPod, a device that works seamlessly with iTunes. Apple has sold almost a million iPods, even though the least expensive one costs $300.

Then Steve had an epiphany: Wouldn't it be awesome if people could buy high-quality audio tracks via the Internet and load them directly into iTunes instead of going to the store to buy CDs to rip? It dawned on him that Apple had all the pieces in place to start such a business. For one thing, the company already had the Apple Store, an online operation selling more than $1 billion a year in computers and software, most of which can be purchased with a single mouse-click. It also runs the Internet's largest movie-trailer downloading site.

The only thing missing was music. Until recently it would have been impossible for a major tech company like Apple to license tunes from Warner, EMI, Universal, Sony, and BMG. Executives at those companies simply didn't trust their peers in the technology world. Many felt—not without some justification—that PC makers promoted piracy because it helped sell computers.

Apple, however, straddles the worlds of technology and entertainment like no other software or hardware maker. Along with running Apple, Jobs is CEO of Pixar, the digital-animation studio whose movies include *Toy Story* and *Monsters, Inc.* He also has plenty of admirers in the music world. Some of Apple's most zealous fans are rock stars who use Macs, both at home and in the recording studio. "Musicians have always adopted Macs," says Trent Reznor of Nine Inch Nails fame. Jobs is enough of a

AMANDA FRIEDMAN

rock star himself—is anybody in the technology world as cool?—that he's been able to get U2's Bono on the phone to discuss the iTunes Music Store. He's personally demonstrated it to Mick Jagger.

The iPod, too, has become a fetish item among musicians and notoriously technophobic music company executives. "I'm addicted to mine," says Interscope Geffen A&M records chairman Jimmy Iovine. It made sense to Iovine and a lot of other record company big shots that if Apple could transform a geeky device like the portable MP3 player into a sexy product with mass-market appeal, it might be able to work similar wonders with online digital-music sales. It's probably no coincidence that the most vocal boosters of the Apple store are Universal and Warner, whose debt-ridden parents—Vivendi and AOL Time Warner, respectively—are under pressure from investors to get out of the music business entirely.

The record companies were still leery enough of Apple that they would agree only to one-year deals with Jobs. Nevertheless, he was able to persuade Universal, EMI, Sony, BMG, and Warner to stop fixating on their subscription models and take a radically different approach to selling digital music. People want to own music, not rent it, Jobs says. "Nobody ever went out and asked users, 'Would you like to keep paying us every month for music that you thought you already bought?' " he scoffs. "The record companies got this crazy idea from some finance person looking at AOL, and then rubbing his hands together and saying, 'I'd sure like to get some of that recurring subscription revenue.' " He adds, "Just watch. We'll have more people using the iTunes Music Store in the first day than Pressplay or MusicNet have even signed up as subscribers—probably in the first hour." We'll let you know in a future issue if that bold prediction proves accurate.

Record company executives aren't ready to dump the subscription model—yet. "I'm not sure subscriptions are going to work," says David Munns, CEO of North American Recorded Music for EMI. "A mixed model where you can rent some music and download what you really like could work. Let's keep an open mind." But what really grabs music executives about iTunes is its sheer simplicity. "It's a lot easier to get people to migrate from physical CDs to buying individual songs online than it is to jump-start a subscription service," says Warner's Ames.

Apple is trying to make that transition as easy as possible. With the iTunes Music Store, you can browse titles by artist, song title, or genre. Songs will be encoded in a new format called AAC, which offers sound quality superior to MP3s—

even those "ripped" at a very high data rate. That means each AAC file takes up a lot less disc space, so you'll be able to squeeze better-quality music, and more of it, onto your computer and iPod. Moreover, each song will have a digital image of the album artwork from the CD on which the track was originally sold. Says Sony's Lack: "I don't think it was more than a 15-second decision in my mind [to license music to Apple] once Steve started talking."

Apple has also come up with a copy-protection scheme that satisfies the music industry but won't alienate paying customers. You can burn individual songs onto an unlimited number of CDs. You can download them onto as many iPods as you might own. In other words, the music is pretty much yours to do with as you please. Casual music pirates, however, won't like it. The iTunes jukebox software will allow a specific playlist of songs or an album to be burned onto a CD 10 times. You can burn more than that only if you manually change the order of the songs in the playlist.

And anybody who tries to upload iTunes Music Store songs onto KaZaA will be shocked. Each song is encrypted with a digital key so that it can be played only on three authorized computers, and that prevents songs from being transferred online. Even if you burn the AAC songs onto a CD that a conventional CD player can read and then re-rip them back into standard MP3 files, the sound quality is awful.

The iTunes Music Store will initially offer 200,000 tunes, paying the record companies an average of 65 cents for each track it sells. Ultimately Jobs hopes to offer millions of songs, including older music that hasn't yet made it to CD. "This industry has been in such a funk," sighs singer Sheryl Crow. "It really needs something like this to get it going again."

If the iTunes Music Store or something like it takes off, that could change how new music is released, marketed, and promoted. Until recently the chief fear in the music industry about letting people buy individual songs via the Internet was that it would kill the album by enabling consumers to cherry-pick their favorite tracks. Music company executives now bravely say that a singles-based business might actually revive sales.

Steve is doing everything he can to stoke their optimism. "Nobody thinks of albums anymore, anyway," he argues, perhaps a little too blithely. "People think of playlists and mixes. We'll still sell albums as artists put them out, but for most consumers of popular music, we think they'll more likely buy single tracks that they like. And then they'll organize them into customized playlists in their computers and on their iPods."

The reality is that initially, at least, the record companies will probably sell less music if they shift to an Internet-based singles business model. For years they have been able to get away with releasing albums with two or three potential hits bundled with ho-hum filler cuts. That has been wonderful for the industry, but it has made a generation of consumers who pay $18.99 for CDs very cynical. "People are sick and tired of that," says singer-songwriter Seal. "That's why people are stealing music."

For some artists, the idea of a singles-driven business is anathema. "There's a flow to a good album," says Nine Inch Nails' Reznor. "The songs support each other. That's the way I like to make music." But Crow says it would be a relief to put out singles instead of producing an entire album every time she wants to reach fans. "It would be nice to have a mechanism to release a song or two or three or four on their own," she says.

A renewed emphasis on individual songs could well improve the quality of music and lead to a reordering of the entire industry. It won't happen overnight, but the record companies had better get used to this new model. Now that Apple has gotten the music industry to support its pay-per-download store, nearly all of its Wintel PC-based rivals say they will augment their subscription businesses with similar offerings. "Steve's pushing the ball forward here," concedes Rob Glaser, CEO of RealNetworks, which owns nearly 40% of MusicNet and plans to purchase Listen.com's well-regarded Rhapsody subscription service.

But Glaser insists that Apple is ignoring a significant part of the digital music market by offering just downloading. He says Rhapsody users spend 72% of their time listening to streaming music. Only 13% pay $1 to burn cuts onto CDs. "If you make a really cool playlist of 200 songs on Rhapsody, you pay only $9.95 a month," he says. "If you use Apple, it's $200. Maybe guys like Steve and me can afford that, but I'm trying to run a service for everyone else too."

NO MATTER WHAT HAPPENS, Jobs will likely sell more Macs. But that's not all he's after with music. The Music Store is his latest effort to diversify Apple's sources of revenue beyond Macs. With Apple's share of the desktop computer market stuck at less than 5% in the U.S. and less than 3% worldwide for several years, the iPod is the most obvious new line of business, steering Apple onto the home turf of consumer electronics giants like Sony and Matsushita. Now Apple makes almost as much operating profit on each iPod it sells as it does on each iMac, even though the iPod costs a fraction as much to manufacture. So it should come as no surprise that Jobs is releasing three new versions of the iPod in conjunction with the Music Store.

Jobs has been very shrewd about the way he moved the iPod into the PC universe. Anyone who has tried the iPod with both systems will tell you it's a lot more fun to use if you plug it into a Mac running Apple's OS X than into a Dell with Windows XP. "The Windows iPod sucks" is Seal's appraisal. "But what they are really doing is trying to get people to wonder, 'Hmm, should I switch over?'" Jobs is betting that the iTunes Music Store, like the iPod, could be just such a Trojan horse.

It's not as easy as it sounds. How many Windows iPod owners know what they're missing by not using OS X? Do any of them really care? Perhaps that's why Jobs is rolling out iTunes for Windows too. In fact, Warner's Roger Ames is trying to broker a deal in which AOL would adopt iTunes as its music-management software. "Steve was resistant at first," Ames says. "But now I understand that he's decided to go that way." AOL has been trying to develop its own music store to go along with its subscription service but hasn't figured out a billing system for individual tracks, as Apple has. A deal with AOL would land the iTunes Music Store on the desktops of AOL's 26 million subscribers. That could quickly make Apple the dominant seller of digital music on the Internet. AOL would neither confirm nor deny a possible deal.

A big play for Windows users would be a huge shift for a man who has largely created a product—the Mac—that exists in a walled garden cut off from the much vaster PC world. Clearly, Apple will benefit enormously if it boosts its share of the computer market by even 1%; such a gain would lift its revenues by nearly a third and increase profits even more. In the meantime, if the iTunes Music Store takes off and computer users of all stripes start buying millions of songs online each month, that will translate into tens of millions of dollars in new revenues per month for Apple.

His adventures in the music business have led to other changes in Jobs' thinking. During a photo shoot with Sheryl Crow for this article, he acknowledged to the singer that he had never really understood what rap music was all about. But while playing with a prototype of the iTunes Music Store on his Mac at home in recent weeks, he had started downloading some of Eminem's tracks.

"You know, he really is a great poet," Crow said.

To which Steve replied, "Yeah, he's starting to kind of grow on me."

REDUX

SIMPLY IRRESISTIBLE
WHY APPLE IS THE BEST RETAILER IN AMERICA.

*BOX POPULI:
THE APPLE STORE
ON FIFTH AVENUE IN
NEW YORK CITY*

WHEN APPLE opened its first store in 2001, some retailing experts predicted failure. Today the company operates more than 350 outlets around the world. Like other Apple products, the stores are meticulously planned, beautifully designed, and inspire cult-like devotion from fans. Turn the page for a look inside.

"Our goal was never to have a store for a cult. It was to be a store for everyone." —Ron Johnson, Apple senior VP of retail

Annual sales per square foot, in fiscal 2006

Apple Store	$4,032*
Tiffany & Co.	$2,666
Best Buy	$930*
Neiman Marcus	$611
Saks	$362

*Data are for the past 12 months.

SOURCE: SANFORD C. BERNSTEIN

PAUL SAKUMA—AP (JOBS)

THE ARCHITECT

STEVE JOBS, CEO, Apple
VISION: "A buying experience as good as our products."
DETAIL: Holds patent for staircase design
LEFT: Ministore in Palo Alto

THE SOFTWARE

APPLICANTS PER OPENING: 20
HARVARD UNIVERSITY: 10
JOB REQUIREMENTS: Must understand machines and people

THE HARDWARE

MATERIALS: Low-iron glass; bead-blasted stainless steel from Japan; Pietra Serena stone from Italy
DESIGN: Spiral staircase with cylindrical elevator

THE TRAFFIC

WEEKLY VISITORS PER STORE: 13,800
AT FIFTH AVENUE STORE: 50,000-plus
IDEAL LOCATION: "Live there, work there, play there, shop there, tour there."

THE LOOK AND FEEL

PRODUCTS UNDER GLASS: None
PURPOSE: Allow customer to "test drive" new products
NUMBER OF DISPLAY COMPUTERS CONNECTED TO INTERNET: All
NEXT BIG THING: iPhone
IPHONES SOLD THROUGH THIRD PARTIES (EXCEPT CINGULAR): None

INSANELY LUCRATIVE

NUMBER OF APPLE STORES: 174 and counting
FLAGSHIPS: Fifth Avenue (above) and SoHo, **New York City**; **San Francisco**; North Michigan Avenue, **Chicago**; Regent Street, **London**; the Grove, **Los Angeles**; Ginza, **Tokyo**; Shinsaibashi, **Osaka**
UNDER CONSTRUCTION: Boston

The Legacy of Steve Jobs

 Chapter Four

 Charis Tsevis

 Fortune
March 17,
2008

THE TROUBLE WITH STEVE

JOBS LIKES TO MAKE HIS OWN RULES, WHETHER THE TOPIC IS COMPUTERS, STOCK OPTIONS, OR EVEN PANCREATIC CANCER. THE SAME TRAITS THAT MAKE HIM A GREAT CEO DRIVE HIM TO PUT HIS COMPANY, AND HIS INVESTORS, AT RISK.

BY PETER ELKIND

N OCTOBER 2003, as the computer world buzzed about what cool new gadget he would introduce next, Apple CEO Steve Jobs—then presiding over the most dramatic corporate turnaround in the history of Silicon Valley—found himself confronting a life-and-death decision.

During a routine abdominal scan, doctors had discovered a tumor growing in his pancreas. While a diagnosis of pancreatic cancer is often tantamount to a swiftly executed death sentence, a biopsy revealed that Jobs had a rare—and treatable—form of the disease. If the tumor were surgically removed, Jobs' prognosis would be promising: The vast majority of those who underwent the operation survived at least 10 years.

Yet to the horror of the tiny circle of intimates in whom he'd confided, Jobs was considering not having the surgery at all. A Buddhist and vegetarian, the Apple CEO was skeptical of mainstream medicine. Jobs decided to employ alternative methods to treat his pancreatic cancer, hoping to avoid the operation through a special diet—a course of action that hasn't been disclosed until now.

For nine months Jobs pursued this approach, as Apple's board of directors and executive team secretly agonized over the situation—and whether the company needed to disclose anything about its CEO's health to investors. Jobs, after all, was widely viewed as Apple's irreplaceable leader, personally responsible for everything from the creation of the iPod to the selection of the chef in the company cafeteria. News of his illness, especially with an uncertain outcome, would surely send the company's stock reeling. The board decided to say nothing, after seeking advice on its obligations from two outside lawyers, who agreed it could remain silent.

In the end, Jobs had the surgery, on Saturday, July 31, 2004, at Stanford University Medical Center in Palo Alto, near his home. The revelation of his brush with death remained—like everything involving Jobs and Apple—a tightly controlled affair. In fact, nary a word got out until Jobs' tumor had been removed. The next day, in an upbeat e-mail to employees later released to the press, he announced that he had faced a life-threatening illness and was "cured." Jobs assured everyone that he'd be back on the job in September. When trading resumed a day after the announcement, Apple shares fell just 2.4%.

Apple entertained no further questions about Jobs' health, citing the CEO's need for privacy. No one learned just how long Jobs had been sick—or that he had contemplated not having the surgery at all. "It was very traumatic for all of us," recalls one of those in whom Jobs confided, speaking on condition of anonymity because of the topic's sensitivity. "We all really care about Steve, and it was a serious risk for the company as well. It was a very emotional and very difficult time. This was one page in the adventure."

HE STEVE JOBS ADVENTURE: By now it's one of the most remarkable stories in business. When Jobs returned in 1997 to Apple—then facing its own near-death experience—he arrived with a tarnished legend. He was, of course, the charismatic boy wonder who at age 21 had co-founded Apple with Steve Wozniak in his parents' garage back in 1976. He was worth $200 million by 25, made the cover of *Time* magazine at 26, and was thrown out of the company at age 30, in 1985.

What he's accomplished in the past decade has not just restored Jobs to the Silicon Valley pantheon but elevated him to the status of superstar. On the brink of bankruptcy when he returned, Apple now has a market value of $108

ROBERT YAGER [2]

billion—more than Merck, McDonald's, or Goldman Sachs; $1,000 invested in Apple shares on the day Jobs took over is worth about $36,000 today. And it isn't just Apple and its investors that have benefited from Jobs' executive skill. Pixar, where he served simultaneously as CEO, has come to dominate the animation business, churning out mega-hits like *Finding Nemo* and *The Incredibles* that prompted Disney to buy the company in 2006 for $7.5 billion. (Jobs now owns 7.3% of Disney, worth $4.6 billion, in addition to Apple stock worth $682 million.)

No less an authority than Jack Welch has called Jobs "the most successful CEO today." Jobs, at age 53, has even become a global cultural guru, shaping what entertainment we watch, how we listen to music, and what sort of objects we use to work and play. He has changed the game for entire industries.

Jobs is also among the most controversial figures in business. He oozes smug superiority, lacing his public comments with ridicule of Apple's rivals, which he casts as mediocre, evil, and—worst of all—lacking taste. No CEO is more willful or more brazen at making his own rules, in ways both good and bad. And no CEO is more personally identi-fied with—and controlling of—the day-to-day affairs of his business. Even now, Jobs views himself less as a mogul than as an artist, Apple's creator-in-chief. He has listed himself as "co-inventor" on 103 separate Apple patents, everything from the user interface for the iPod to the support system for the glass staircase used in Apple's dazzling retail stores.

Jobs' product introductions are semiannual events, com-plete with packed houses, breathless blog dispatches, and celebrity appearances—two hours of marketing performance art. Who else could have the nation panting in anticipation of a cellphone? After watching Jobs unveil the iPhone, Alan Kay, a personal-computer pioneer who has worked with him, put it this way: "Steve understands desire."

Jobs' personal abuses are also legend: He parks his Mer-cedes in handicapped spaces, periodically reduces subordi-nates to tears, and fires employees in angry tantrums. Yet many of his top deputies at Apple have worked with him for years, and even some of those who have departed say that although it's often brutal and Jobs hogs the credit, they've never done better work.

How Jobs pulls all this off—how this bundle of conflict-ing behaviors can coexist, to spectacular effect, in a single human being—remains a puzzle, even though more than a dozen books have been written about him. Jobs is notorious-ly secretive and controlling when it comes to his relation-ship with the press, and he tries to stifle stories that haven't received his blessing with threats and cajolery.

This story is one of them. While Jobs agreed to be in-terviewed by my colleague Betsy Morris on the subject of Apple's selection as America's Most Admired Company (for the interview portion of this article, see "What Makes Apple Golden"), he refused to comment for this story, which had been in the works for months. Dozens of people who work or have worked with Jobs did agree to extensive interviews, most insisting on not being named (even if praising him) for fear of incurring his anger.

History, of course, is littered with tales of combustible geniuses. What's astounding is how well Jobs has performed atop a large public company—by its nature a collaborative enterprise. Pondering this issue, Stanford management-sci-ence professor Robert Sutton discussed Jobs in his bestsell-ing 2007 book, *The No Asshole Rule: Building a Civilized Workplace and Surviving One That Isn't.* "As soon as people heard I was writing a book on assholes, they would come up to me and start telling a Steve Jobs story," says Sutton. "The degree to which people in Silicon Valley are afraid of Jobs is unbelievable. He made people feel terrible; he made people cry. But he was almost always right, and even when he was wrong, it was so creative it was still amazing." Says Palo Alto venture capitalist Jean-Louis Gassée, a former Apple execu-tive who once worked with Jobs: "Democracies don't make great products. You need a competent tyrant."

Fair enough. But it is also important to understand the ways in which Jobs' attempts to manipulate his world pose risks for Apple—and thus its investors. They are evident in his difficult partnerships with music and television compa-nies, which chafe at his insistence on setting uniform prices for their songs and videos on iTunes; in the real story of his battle with cancer; and in his deployment of stock options at Apple and Pixar, which exposed both companies to backdat-ing scandals.

Jobs himself judges the world in binary terms. Prod-ucts, in his view, are "insanely great" or "shit." One is facing death from cancer or "cured." Subordinates are geniuses or "bozos," indispensable or no longer relevant. People in his orbit regularly flip, at a second's notice, from one category to another, in what early Apple colleagues came to call his "hero-shithead roller coaster."

Jobs' own story is far more complex. And in the 26 years that *Fortune* has been ranking America's Most Admired Companies, never has the corporation at the head of the list so closely resembled a one-man show. Last year Piper Jaffray analyst Gene Munster opined that if Jobs were forced out as a result of the backdating scandal, Apple's shares would drop 20% overnight. At the company's current market cap, that would make him Apple's $22 billion man. "Steve Jobs running the company from jail would be better for the stock price than Steve Jobs not being CEO," muses Sutton.

Jobs is hardly likely to be forced out, as we shall see. On the contrary, he's likely to continue taking Apple—and its customers, competitors, and investors—on a wild ride to places they couldn't have imagined.

It may be instructive, then, to consider what drives the Steve Jobs adventure.

JOBS' CONFIDENTIAL PHONE LIST from the mid-1980s at Apple Computer, included in more than 500 boxes of company documents archived at Stanford, reveals the rarefied air in which he operated while still in his 20s. There are private listings for Joan Baez and Diane Keaton (both onetime romantic interests), the home phone for California governor Jerry Brown, and the White House line for Richard Darman, one of President Reagan's top aides. By then, Jobs was already one of the first true business celebrities.

Jobs' phone list also reflected the complex crosscurrents of his personal life. There were Kobun Chino, the Zen Buddhist monk who was his spiritual guru and would later preside at his wedding; Clara and Paul Jobs, the working-class California couple who had adopted and raised him; Joanne Simpson, his biological mother, whom he'd tracked down as an adult with the help of a private detective; and his first serious girlfriend, Chrisann Brennan, the mother of Lisa, his out-of-wedlock daughter.

There was no listing, however, for Abdulfattah "John" Jandali, his Syrian biological father—a man Jobs has never discussed publicly. Jobs was born to Jandali and Simpson, a pair of 23-year-old unwed University of Wisconsin graduate students, in 1955. Just months after giving their baby up for adoption, the two married, then had another child, whom they kept: Mona Simpson, who grew up to become a critically acclaimed novelist and never knew her famous brother existed until she was an adult.

A charming, promising academic, Jandali later abandoned his wife and 4-year-old daughter, moving from job to job as a political science professor before leaving academe. Now 76, he works as food and beverage director at the Boomtown Hotel & Casino near Reno. Mona Simpson's novel, *The Lost Father*, is based on her quest to find him.

When Jobs had his own illegitimate child, also at the age of 23, he too struggled with his responsibilities. For two years, though already wealthy, he denied paternity while Lisa's mother went on welfare. At one point Jobs even swore

in a signed court document that he couldn't be Lisa's father because he was "sterile and infertile, and as a result thereof, did not have the physical capacity to procreate a child." He later acknowledged paternity of Lisa, married Laurene Powell, a Stanford MBA, and fathered three more children. Lisa Brennan-Jobs, now 29, graduated from Harvard and is a writer.

At Apple during his 20s, Jobs served as board chairman and head of the Macintosh division. But he was never given the CEO job. Adult supervision—in the form of professional managers—was recruited to run the fast-growing business, notably Pepsi president John Sculley. "Back then he was uncontrollable," venture capitalist Arthur Rock, an early Apple board member, told *Institutional Investor* last year. "He got ideas in his head, and the hell with what anybody else wanted to do. Being a founder of the company, he went off and did them regardless of whether it ended up being good for the company."

To be sure, many of the gifts that would drive Apple's resurrection over the past decade were already evident in the 1980s: the marketing showmanship, the inspirational summons to "put a dent in the universe," the siren call to talent. Engineer Bob Belleville recalls Jobs recruiting him from Xerox in 1982 with the words, "I hear you're great, but everything you've done so far is crap. Come work for me." Jobs famously seduced Sculley to Apple by challenging him: "Do you want to spend the rest of your life selling sugared water, or do you want a chance to change the world?"

But after two years of working closely with Jobs, Sculley came to liken him to Russian revolutionary Leon Trotsky. In *Odyssey*, his memoir of this period, he called Jobs "a zealot, his vision so pure that he couldn't accommodate that vision to the imperfections of the world." In 1985, Sculley orchestrated Jobs' firing after a power struggle. And in his memoir, Sculley dismissed Jobs' vision for the company. "Apple was supposed to become a wonderful consumer products company," Sculley wrote. "This was a lunatic plan. High tech could not be designed and sold as a consumer product."

Of course, Sculley was dead wrong.

DURING THE ENSUING 12 "wilderness years," as they have come to be known, Jobs started Next Computing and bought what became Pixar from George Lucas. Next was a business failure, burning through hundreds of millions in investors' money. But by the time Apple bought Next in 1997, setting in motion Jobs' return, he obviously had developed the capacity to become a CEO for the ages.

Apple was on the ropes. Right away, Jobs dug into the mucky details of the business, creating a sense of urgency,

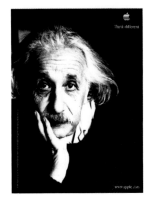

COURTESY GASLIGHT AD ARCHIVE [3]

THINK DIFFERENT: JOBS CONCEIVES OF HIMSELF AS THE COMPANY'S CREATOR-IN-CHIEF. HIS ARTISTIC SENSIBILITY EXTENDS TO EVERYTHING APPLE DOES, INCLUDING ITS MEMORABLE ADVERTISING CAMPAIGNS.

radically reducing Apple's product line, and accelerating a wholesale cost cutting that would shrink the company back to profitability. Jobs had become a far better leader, less of a go-to-hell aesthete who cared only about making beautiful objects. Now he was a go-to-hell aesthete who cared about making beautiful objects that made money. No engineering spec, no design flourish was too small for his scrutiny. "It wasn't like he was some mythical creative genius and leaving the rest of the company to itself," says retired DuPont chairman Ed Woolard, a former director who was instrumental in bringing Jobs back. "It may have been true in the past. It was not true when he came back. He clearly was deeply involved in all the practical operations of Apple."

That's not to suggest that he ever became easy to work for. Jobs is even known to yell at company directors. Asked how she dealt with her boss, former Apple PR chief Laurence Clavere once told a colleague that before heading into a meeting with Jobs, she embraced the mindset of a bullfighter entering the ring: "I pretend I'm already dead." (Clavere says today that she doesn't recall making the comparison but notes that "working with Steve is incredibly challenging, incredibly interesting. It was also sometimes incredibly difficult.") Jobs' break-the-rules attitude extends to refusing to put a license plate on his Mercedes. "It's a little game I play," he explained to *Fortune* in 2001.

Often Jobs would suddenly "flip," taking an idea that he'd mocked (maybe your idea) and embracing it passionately— and as his own—without ever acknowledging that his view had changed. "He has this ability to change his mind and completely forget his old opinion about something," says a former close colleague who asked not to be named. "It's weird. He can say, 'I love white; white is the best.' And then three months later say, 'Black is the best; white is not the best.' He doesn't live with his mistake. It evaporates." Jobs would rationalize it all by simply explaining, "We're doing what's right today."

Despite all that, Jobs was able to put together a world-class team when he got back to Apple. He assembled an inner circle dominated by his brain trust from Next, which included his two top product guys: Avie Tevanian, who ran software, and Jon Rubinstein, who presided over the hard-

ware team. Phil Schiller, already at Apple, was promoted to head of product marketing, while operations chief Tim Cook (now Apple's COO) was recruited from Compaq. Jobs hired Ron Johnson from Target to launch Apple's retail stores.

The group also included two executives who would later bear the brunt of Apple's backdating scandal. The first was general counsel Nancy Heinen, who had also come over from Next. Dominique Trempont, Next's former CFO, recalls that when Jobs was first considering whether to hire Heinen there, he asked to see some of the contracts she had written so that he could evaluate the "aesthetics" of her work. The second executive was the lone holdover from the previous regime, Fred Anderson, chief financial officer and the company's de facto No. 2. Anderson was widely credited with keeping Apple alive long enough to give Jobs time to work his magic. A calm, square-faced, retired Air Force officer, Anderson dealt with liquidity crises, restructurings, Wall Street—and the always volatile CEO. One former board member described Anderson's role as "tantrum controller."

To keep all this talent, Jobs took a typical Silicon Valley step: He eliminated most cash bonuses from executive compensation and started handing out lots more stock options instead. And here, as elsewhere, Jobs played by his own rules.

AMONG THE FIRST THINGS Jobs did in 1997 was to reprice underwater stock options for all Apple employees, twice in six months. Apple also made a big grant in a way that looked like "springloading," issuing options one day before the announcement of a big deal with Microsoft sent Apple shares soaring 33%.

Repricing and springloading are controversial (they give insiders an edge that shareholders don't enjoy), but they are not illegal. Neither is it illegal to grant "in-the-money" options with a below-market price as long as the action is disclosed and accounted for. What is illegal, though, is backdating—the picking of a date in the past, when a stock's value was lower, to assign the exercise price of options—without those adjustments. Backdating invariably involves lying to investors, creating false documentation, and avoiding the earnings hit required for giving employees in-the-money grants.

In 2006, after the *Wall Street Journal* ran its Pulitzer Prize–winning series about backdated stock options, Apple (which hadn't been named in the coverage) scrambled to assess whether it had a problem. The company appointed a special board committee to investigate, which concluded that it did. The company discovered "irregularities" with 6,428 grants between 1997 and 2001—roughly one in six that Apple issued during that period. (New disclosure requirements after that time caused backdating to dry up.) The company also found no instances of backdating before Jobs took over as CEO. Apple was forced to restate its earnings, taking a pretax charge for unreported compensation expenses of $105 million.

Disney, which bought Pixar in 2006, also investigated and found a backdating problem there during Jobs' time as CEO. As the *Wall Street Journal* first reported, key Pixar executives received options grants priced at the stock's yearly low in 1997, 1998, 2000, and 2003. A Merrill Lynch analyst put the odds of that happening by chance at one in 112 million. (Disney declined to comment on backdating.)

But the events at the two companies don't quite fit the classic backdating template, which has cost dozens of executives their jobs. For one thing, Jobs didn't personally benefit from backdated options—at least not directly. For another, in a climate where many were rushing to judgment, Jobs enjoyed the benefit of the doubt from protective boards.

Was Jobs himself involved in backdating stock options? At Apple, the answer is yes: In an SEC filing, Apple acknowledged that Jobs "was aware [of] or recommended the selection of some favorable grant dates." But Apple's investigation concluded that Jobs' involvement didn't amount to misconduct because he "was unaware of the accounting implications." As for Pixar, Disney issued a four-sentence summary of its own internal inquiry, concluding that "while options were backdated at Pixar" before its sale to Disney, "no one currently associated with the Company engaged in any intentional or deliberate acts of misconduct."

The SEC and the Justice Department are still investigating backdating at both Apple and Pixar. The SEC last April announced that it would take no action against Apple, citing the company's "swift, extensive, and extraordinary cooperation," including its "prompt self-reporting, an independent internal investigation, the sharing of the results of that investigation with the government, and the implementation of new controls designed to prevent the recurrence of fraudulent conduct."

At the same time, the SEC filed charges against two former members of Jobs' inner circle—general counsel Heinen and CFO Anderson. Heinen, accused of orchestrating two backdated grants and falsifying documentation for them, has pleaded innocent to fraud claims and is preparing for trial. Anderson has settled a lesser claim of negligence involving one grant, paying $3.64 million in disgorgement and fines, while remaining free to serve as an officer or director of public companies (he chairs the audit committee at eBay).

Anderson, in an extraordinary public statement he issued after settling his case with the SEC, disputed Apple's exoneration of Jobs. Through his lawyer, he said he alerted Jobs to the accounting implications even as the CEO was in the process of picking a retroactive date for the grant to his top lieutenants. He also said Jobs assured him that the award had been properly approved by Apple's board.

THE STORY OF THAT GRANT opens in late 2000, a panicky time for Apple. Silicon Valley was reeling from the dotcom crash. Apple had missed its quarterly numbers, and after a big run-up in the company's stock (multiplying the company's market cap from $2 billion to $16 billion), Apple's market value had melted back down to $5 billion. Jobs feared that his inner circle was ripe for poaching.

In October 2000, Jobs started talking to the directors about giving the executive team a big grant to place them in golden handcuffs. At the time—for 15 months, in fact—Apple's board had no compensation committee providing oversight over the CEO's grant practices, an extremely unusual situation. (Almost 99% of public companies at the time had compensation committees, according to a study by the research firm ISS, a unit of RiskMetrics.)

In late 2000, Jobs told at least one of his top lieutenants to expect the options to be priced on Jan. 2, 2001. But at the end of January, Jobs was still consulting with Heinen about the grant. The stock had been climbing that month, which meant that options would have a higher exercise price than if they had been granted on Jan. 2.

On Jan. 30, 2001, according to the SEC's suit, Heinen e-mailed Jobs with a list of possible retroactive dates for the grant; Anderson got the list too. The goal was to get the executive team a price almost as low as the close on Jan. 2. (Heinen thought that using the original date might draw public criticism for springloading because Apple stock had jumped just a few days later on product announcements by Jobs at Macworld.)

Jobs picked Jan. 17 for the executive-team grant, a date when Apple shares still had a nice low closing price. According to the SEC suit, Heinen instructed a staff attorney, Wendy Howell, to prepare a "unanimous written consent" (UWC) for the signature of Apple board members, retroactively approving the options with "an effective date of Jan. 17, 2001, priced at [$8.41]." (All share prices and numbers of options in this story are adjusted for subsequent splits in Apple stock.)

The board members didn't fax back the signed papers for the executive-team stock-options grant until Feb. 7—which, in the SEC's view, made that the proper grant date. By then, Apple stock was up 23% over the Jan. 17 grant price. This meant each of the six executives receiving options got a paper windfall of either $1.6 million or $3.9 million, depending on the size of their grant. According to the SEC, it also meant Apple had engaged in illegal backdating, awarding in-the-money options without disclosing it and inflating company earnings by failing to record the $18.9 million expense on its financial statements.

Apple directors, like the company, refused to make any public comment for this story. But in response to shareholder lawsuits, Apple's lawyers argued that the directors routinely signed UWCs giving perfunctory approval to option grants they'd effectively delegated to management. Similarly, the lawyers argued, Jobs had no reason to think there was a problem, because his CFO and general counsel had signed off on the grant.

As a condition of taking over in 1997, Jobs had fired most of Apple's board, installing a new one with just six members. Only two directors were holdovers: Edgar Woolard, the retired DuPont chairman, and Gareth Chang, senior vice president of Hughes Electronics. The others were Oracle CEO Larry Ellison, a close friend of Jobs'; Intuit CEO Bill Campbell, who had worked at Apple back in the 1980s and was Jobs' neighbor; Jerry York, a former CFO of IBM and Chrysler, who later became CEO of Micro Warehouse, a computer reseller that did extensive business with Apple; and Jobs himself.

Apple's board has drawn criticism from governance experts for years. In his 2002 book, *Take On the Street*, former SEC chairman Arthur Levitt complained that Apple's governing body simply failed to meet "good-governance litmus tests." Levitt wrote, "It's plain to me that Apple's board is not designed to act independently of the CEO." A self-described "Apple junkie," Levitt had actually been invited by Jobs to become an Apple director in February 2001—only to be "disinvited" after returning from a visit to Silicon Valley. "Arthur, I don't think you'd be happy on our board, and I think it best if we not invite you," Levitt recounts Jobs telling him in a phone call. Levitt says Jobs explained that he had come to this conclusion after reading a Levitt speech on corporate governance. "Frankly, I think some of the issues you raised, while appropriate for some companies, really don't apply to

Apple's culture," Jobs told him. Levitt says he was "floored."

No question, Apple's culture at this level was out of the ordinary. Jobs accepted a salary of $1 a year. In January 2000, after the stock had soared and the company's survival seemed assured, Apple announced that it was buying Jobs a jet—not a corporate jet for him to use, mind you, but his own Gulfstream V. Total cost to the company, including Jobs' taxes on the gift: $88 million. While the plane has long been cast as a board's creative gesture of gratitude, Woolard says Jobs is the one who thought of it. "He brought up the idea: 'What I really need is a plane where I can take my family to Hawaii on vacation, go to the East Coast.' I said, 'All right.'" Larry Ellison declared, "With what he's done, we ought to give him five airplanes!"

Jobs also got a mega-grant of 40 million options—almost 6% of the company, priced at $21.80 a share. Half would vest immediately, the rest within 18 months. That was unusual, but the board reasoned that it should make up for the 30 months when Jobs had worked for a buck a year.

J OBS' OWN OPTIONS would lead to the second SEC problem for Apple, though only Heinen would face charges for it. The issue arose after the dotcom crash sent Apple's stock price back below $10, and the Apple board, eager to keep Jobs happy, voted on Aug. 29, 2001, to give him a fresh batch of 15 million options at $8.92. But Jobs—sensitive to press criticism he'd been receiving for his 2000 mega-grant, which was underwater—refused to accept the new award unless the board canceled his previous one. Accounting complications that made it impractical to do this—as well as wrangling over the vesting schedule—dragged the matter out until December.

That created a fresh problem: How to price Jobs' award? The stock had climbed since the original board vote back in August, and using that date wouldn't have withstood scrutiny, because Apple was now in a new fiscal year. After Heinen reviewed a spreadsheet showing closing prices for a three-month period with Arthur Levinson, a member of Apple's reconstituted comp committee and the CEO of Genentech, the grant was dated on Oct. 19.

The grant's strike price ($9.15) wouldn't be as good as it was back in August, but it was better than the $10.51 the stock hit on Dec. 18—which, according to the SEC, was the proper price for the grant. Levinson informed the board about the arrangements in an e-mail, noting that he had instructed Heinen to make sure Apple was "conforming to all legal requirements/guidelines."

It wasn't. The SEC claims that Heinen ordered Howell to

dummy up the necessary paperwork to make it look like the full board approved the grant at a special meeting on Oct. 19—a meeting that never took place. Heinen denies this, blaming her subordinate for creating the phony documents.

All this gave Jobs a paper backdating windfall of about $20 million, according to the SEC. But he never cashed in the options, and in March 2003, after Apple's share price kept dropping, Jobs traded his entire stake of 55 million underwater options for the certainty of 10 million restricted shares. In perfect hindsight, given Apple's soaring stock price since that time, he lost a fortune on the deal. Jobs' restricted shares would sell today for about $1.2 billion before taxes. His options, had he kept them, would yield about $5.8 billion (pretax).

Pixar's board did have a compensation committee, but it never met. In fact, the entire Pixar board—also handpicked by Jobs—typically met only about three times a year. Jobs personally negotiated options awards with key executives.

The biggest such grant at issue—2 million options—had gone to *Toy Story* director John Lasseter, Pixar's star creative executive, as part of the 10-year contract he had negotiated with Jobs in 2001. Jobs never received Pixar options himself, but he owned more than half the company, and locking up Lasseter led Disney to buy Pixar in 2006, in an enormously lucrative deal for Jobs that made him Disney's largest shareholder.

Joe Graziano, the former Apple CFO who served on the Pixar board from 1995 until the Disney sale, acknowledges that Lasseter was "the single biggest asset at Pixar." He blames any backdating problems on "an administrative glitch," delaying the completion of paperwork authorizing grants that Jobs had promised. "It was normal for him to come into the board and say, 'This is what we want to do for compensation. We got these two guys. We want to give them these shares and lock them up.' And the board said, 'Go for it.' But unfortunately the documents get signed months later."

That, of course, means the grants were issued improperly. And "glitches" don't explain how grants to the company's most valuable players could be issued at the lowest annual stock price in four separate years.

Pixar, by the time of the backdating disclosures, was no longer a public company but a Disney subsidiary and had no board of its own. At Apple, however, shareholder activists have expressed dismay with the way the company has dealt with the matter. Jobs did issue a brief statement that promised remedial measures and said, "I apologize to Apple's shareholders and employees for these problems, which happened on my watch." But beyond its initial press

THE ART OF ANIMATION: JOBS WITH HIS WIFE, LAURENE POWELL, AT NEW YORK CITY'S MUSEUM OF MODERN ART FOR A PIXAR EXHIBIT

release and a limited elaboration in a subsequent SEC filing, Apple explained nothing about how the backdating had occurred and demanded repayment from no one.

In a detailed report to Apple investors, ISS criticized the board's lack of candor, stating, "Steve Jobs has been instrumental in creating significant shareholder value; however, a cult-like devotion to any CEO can be a huge downside risk to shareholders." Glass Lewis, another shareholder advisory firm, described the special committee findings absolving Jobs as "an attempt to whitewash the backdating scandal."

At Apple's annual shareholder meeting last May in Cupertino, the two firms recommended that shareholders withhold their votes for reelecting most of the outside Apple directors. For three of the directors, more than 30% of shareholders did. By the rubber-stamp standards of such proceedings, a 30% vote against directors of a company on a tear—the iPhone was about to go on sale, the stock was headed to the moon—is noteworthy.

WHEN THE CEO of a publicly traded corporation is diagnosed with a serious illness, what is his obligation to inform shareholders? There is no clear answer. The SEC requires that any public company disclose material information to investors so that they can include it in their calculation of whether to buy or sell a stock. But there are no specific guidelines governing health issues, and the SEC has never taken action against a company in this area. It is generally accepted that a company should disclose the diagnosis of a CEO's fatal illness, while it need not say anything about a problem like a broken arm. Everything in between is problematic—and the tension between privacy and shareholder interests is even greater when the CEO is so powerfully identified with the company's fortunes.

Different companies have handled the problem in different ways. When Intel CEO Andy Grove was diagnosed with prostate cancer in 1995, he made no formal disclosure—Grove chose to write about it instead in a 1996 article for *Fortune*. On the other hand, Berkshire Hathaway's Warren

BRIAN ACH—WIREIMAGE.COM/GETTY

Buffett—one of the few *Fortune* 500 CEOs considered as essential to his company as Jobs is to Apple—issued a press release in June 2000 days after he learned he would need surgery to remove benign polyps along with part of his colon, even though the procedure was considered routine.

The story of how Jobs managed his illness has not previously been disclosed. This account comes from several sources with personal knowledge of the situation; all insisted on not being identified.

Jobs' tumor was discovered in October 2003. He had been getting abdominal scans periodically because of a history of intestinal problems. His doctors noticed a growth that turned out to be an islet cell neuroendocrine tumor, a rare and operable form of pancreatic cancer. With surgery, his long-term prognosis would be good.

But Jobs sought instead to treat his tumor with a special diet while launching a lengthy exploration of alternative approaches. "It's safe to say he was hoping to find a solution that would avoid surgery," says one person familiar with the situation. "I don't know if he truly believed that was possible. The odd thing is, for us what seemed like an alternative type of thing, for him is normal. It's not out of the ordinary for Steve."

Apple director Levinson, who has a Ph.D. in biochemistry, monitored the situation for the board. He and another director, Bill Campbell, tried to persuade Jobs to have the surgery. "There was genuine concern on the part of several board members that he may not have been doing the best thing for his health," says one insider. "But Steve is Steve. He can be pretty stubborn."

By the standards of medical science, it was an open-and-shut case: There was no serious alternative to surgery. "Surgery is the only treatment modality that can result in cure," Dr. Jeffrey Norton, chief of surgical oncology at Stanford, wrote in a 2006 medical journal article about this kind of pancreatic cancer. It was Norton, one of the foremost experts in the field, who eventually operated on the Apple CEO, *Fortune* is told. (He declined to comment.)

Dr. Roderich Schwarz, chairman of surgical oncology at the University of Texas Southwestern Medical Center in Dallas, who has performed the procedure more than 150 times (but who was not involved in Jobs' case), says that waiting more than a few weeks with this diagnosis "makes no sense because you don't know what the potential for growth or spread is." Schwarz says he knows of no evidence that diet can be helpful. "But the patient decides. If they believe an herbal diet can do miracles, they have to make the decision. Every once in a while you have somebody who decides something you wish they wouldn't."

The surgery Jobs faced, known as the "Whipple procedure," is brutal and complex. It lasts six hours or more and involves removing parts of the pancreas, bile duct, and intestines, then reconstructing the digestive tract. But it's relatively safe: Mortality from the surgery is less than 5% at specialized medical centers with surgeons who have performed it many times.

Jobs put the procedure off for more than nine months, raising the thorny issue of disclosure. He told the board, and the board decided to say nothing. Palo Alto attorney Larry Sonsini, the company's longtime outside counsel, advised the directors that the CEO's right to privacy trumped any disclosure requirement as long as he could continue to perform his duties. A second outside lawyer agreed. So Apple conducted business as usual, disclosing nothing and letting the tiny circle of insiders who knew about the situation continue to trade Apple shares.

The board of Pixar, the other public company where Jobs served as CEO, remained in the dark until his announcement, according to director Graziano. "All I know is I didn't [know]," Graziano told *Fortune*.

In the end Jobs had the surgery, at the end of July in 2004. Sources tell *Fortune* that he decided to proceed with the operation earlier that month, after a scan revealed growth in the tumor. By all accounts, the surgery was a success.

It is impossible to know whether Jobs' decision to delay the procedure has increased his risk of a cancer recurrence in any way. In a newspaper interview, Norton estimated that 80% to 90% of patients with Jobs' condition survived at least 10 years, while cautioning that predictions are difficult because the number of cases is so small.

Jobs himself has never volunteered much on the matter—except once. In a June 2005 commencement address he gave at Stanford University, he described the sequence of events this way: "About a year ago, I was diagnosed with cancer. I had a scan at 7:30 in the morning, and it clearly showed a tumor on my pancreas... The doctors told me this was almost certainly a type of cancer that is incurable, and that I should expect to live no longer than three to six months... Later that evening I had a biopsy where they stuck an endoscope down my throat, through my stomach into my intestines, put a needle into my pancreas and got a few cells from the tumor. I was sedated, but my wife, who was there, told me that when they viewed the cells under a microscope, the doctor started crying, because it turned out to be a very rare form of pancreatic cancer that is curable with surgery. I had the surgery, and, thankfully, I am fine now."

It was a great speech, simple and moving—though it

clearly left the false impression that Jobs had learned of his illness in mid-2004 and immediately proceeded to surgery, when in fact he had learned of it in October 2003.

Ralph Whitworth, an activist institutional investor, served as chairman of Waste Management when its CEO was stricken with a fatal brain tumor. He says the issue is "a very tricky one," but Apple should have disclosed Jobs' illness promptly after assessing his situation—whether legally required to or not. "Good governance has nothing to do with following the minimum standards," says Whitworth. "Executives should announce before they're going into major surgery. Yes, your stock will go down. [But] how would the shareholders have felt if they said he died on the operating table?"

Former SEC chairman Levitt agrees. "It's a difficult personal decision," says Levitt. "But clearly if a CEO is going in for major surgery, that's a disclosable item."

In the end, the combination of a happy outcome and remarkable secrecy about just how long Apple had known Jobs was sick minimized any public criticism—or impact on its shares. "Steve came through this okay, and Apple never suffered because of it," says one insider. "Had it come out differently—thank God it didn't—there could have been a lot of people second-guessing Apple had they known what happened."

LAST YEAR THE FOUNDER of the *Stanford Social Innovation Review* called Apple one of "America's Least Philanthropic Companies." Jobs had terminated all of Apple's long-standing corporate philanthropy programs within weeks after returning to Apple in 1997, citing the need to cut costs until profitability rebounded. But the programs have never been restored.

Unlike Bill Gates—the tech world's other towering figure—Jobs has not shown much inclination to hand over the reins of his company to create a different kind of personal legacy. While his wife is deeply involved in an array of charitable projects, Jobs' only serious foray into personal philanthropy was short-lived. In January 1987, after launching Next, he also, without fanfare or public notice, incorporated the Steven P. Jobs Foundation. "He was very interested in food and health issues and vegetarianism," recalls Mark Vermilion, the community affairs executive Jobs hired to run it. Vermilion persuaded Jobs to focus on "social entrepreneurship" instead. But the Jobs foundation never did much of anything besides hiring famed graphic designer Paul Rand to design its logo. (Explains Vermilion: "He wanted a logo worthy of his expectations.") Jobs shut down the foundation after less than 15 months.

JOBS HAS NEVER REVEALED any plans to leave Apple, though after news of his pancreatic cancer was disclosed, the board insisted it had privately discussed a succession plan. It is hard to imagine a tougher act to follow. Indeed, Jobs is a tough act for even Jobs to follow.

Already in 2008, Jobs has unveiled his usual array of sleek new products, highlighted by the MacBook Air, billed as "the world's thinnest notebook." The company's most recent quarterly results were its best ever: Apple reported $1.58 billion in profit, $18 billion in the bank, and zero debt. Despite signs of a recession, the company projected second-quarter earnings growth of 29%.

But this time, all that just wasn't amazing enough. Since the beginning of 2008, Apple shares have tumbled by 40% from their all-time high in late December (in a down market, to be sure). Disappointing the masses is a risk you take when your stock is priced for bedazzlement.

And even for Apple, conjuring the magic won't get any easier. It's hard for a big company to keep growing rapidly, especially if the economy heads into a downturn. Cellphone makers—and even Google—are cranking out new products to compete with the iPhone. The iPod market shows signs of being saturated. Amazon's new digital-music store is gunning for iTunes, aided by record companies eager to escape Jobs' insistence on dictating the price for their content. It's the same reason NBC Universal took its shows off iTunes. Then there's the possibility of additional fallout from the SEC and Justice Department investigations at Apple and Pixar.

As usual, Apple's fortunes will rest not just on external factors, but on the shoulders of its CEO, who has pushed his company both to astounding heights and to the edge of significant risk. It is Steve Jobs himself who is the wonder—as well as the worry.

Editor's note: The SEC ultimately took no action against Apple, Pixar, or Steve Jobs in its investigations of stock-options backdating. Former Apple general counsel Nancy Heinen settled with the SEC in August 2008, agreeing to pay $2.2 million without admitting to or denying the government's charges. Under the agreement, Heinen was also barred from serving as an officer or director of a public company for five years, and suspended from appearing before the SEC for three years. Heinen and former Apple CFO Fred Anderson (who settled earlier) were the only individuals charged in the backdating investigations at Apple and Pixar.

FOUR PEOPLE WHO RARELY SPEAK PUBLICLY ABOUT JOBS EXPLAIN WHAT MAKES HIM ONE OF THE BEST BUSINESS MINDS OF OUR TIME.

Ralph de la Vega
President and CEO,
AT&T Mobility

WHEN I FIRST SAW THE IPHONE, even though it wasn't in its final state, I was blown away by what Steve had been able to put into that device. He'd found a way to squeeze the Mac OS X operating system into a handheld device. That's when the light bulb went off for me—this device was going to change the industry forever. And it has. It's made the U.S. the epicenter of smartphone development.
—Interview by Stephanie N. Mehta

Bob Iger
CEO,
Disney

WHEN I THINK OF STEVE, the word "friend" comes first. Second, he is an incredible sounding board. We recently decided to revamp our Disney stores, and his contribution, very early in the process, was to ask that we create a statement—in other words, ask ourselves, "What do you want the stores to say to people when they walk in?" He didn't tell us what it would be, but he told us it was necessary that we have one. Another piece of valuable advice he gave to me was to build a prototype of the new store on your property—don't put it in a mall or on the street—build it close enough so that you can visit it often, massage it, and learn from it. And when you're really ready, roll it out.

One remarkable thing about Steve is how he sets expectations on people. I worked for [the legendary ABC News chairman] Roone Arledge for 10 years. He demanded perfection, never accepted mediocrity. Steve is the same. I see that in the way he manages his people. He sets expectations for quality, challenging the status quo—and never accepts no for an answer.
—Interview by Richard Siklos

Jimmy Iovine
Founder and chairman,
Interscope Records

WHATEVER ANYONE SAYS about Apple, if it wasn't for Steve Jobs there would be no legitimate music online. Everybody was lost. The record labels were frozen. When he came up with iTunes, it gave us a [legal] way to get the license ready to go online. Before iTunes, Napster was out of business for two or three years, and then Kazaa and other file-sharing started. There was no legitimate way to buy music. I think his impact on music has been extraordinary.
—Interview by Jon Fortt

Bill Campbell
Chairman and former CEO,
Intuit

I'VE NEVER SEEN HIM not intense. I've known him since 1983. I started at Apple then, as the vice president of marketing, and now I sit on its board. There hasn't been a day in Steve's life that he doesn't get up, think about the company he works for or what he's going to do next. These are things that drive him. He is a wonderful husband and a wonderful father, but his life is all about doing this kind of thing. He wants to create something that has value, that has a legacy. "Legacy" is my word. I'm not sure he ever thinks about legacy. He's just driven like that.

The biggest thing for me was to watch him hire. He's a terrific interviewer. He understands what he wants, and he knows how to get great people. And if you take a look at his management team after 12 years, some are still there, some are gone, but in every [position, you'll find] a high-quality person.

When you watched how the company performed without him, I think the durability of what he created was pretty evident. Who knows what it would look like if he had stayed away longer? As close as I am, I don't even know. But I know that his coming back puts real excitement into the product-development process.
—Interview by Adam Lashinsky

FROM LEFT: DAVID BECKER—REUTERS/CORBIS; FRANK TRAPPER—CORBIS; MICHAEL TRAN—FILMMAGIC/GETTY

Chapter Five

EPILOGUE

What legacy will Steve Jobs leave Apple? For one, a new corporate headquarters, called iSpaceship, that will house nearly 13,000 employees. This futuristic behemoth, enveloped in giant sheets of curved glass, has the elegance and pizzazz of so many other Apple creations. Yet, more important, Jobs hoped that the institution he has left behind will carry his DNA and continue to deliver one blockbuster hit after another. And finally, a fond farewell to one of history's great CEOs.

SJ—CONTOUR BY GETTY

JOBS AT HIS HOME IN PALO ALTO IN 2004. **PHOTOGRAPH BY DIANA WALKER**

STEVE JOBS' REAL LEGACY: APPLE INC. WITHOUT HYPE OR FANFARE, STEVE JOBS HAS BEEN QUIETLY MAKING SURE HIS BELOVED COMPANY IS BUILT TO LAST. BY MIGUEL HELFT

The
Jobs Era

Apple's annual sales
and profits going
back to 1997,
the year Steve Jobs
returned as CEO.

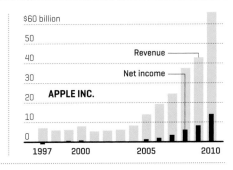

APPLE INC.

THE LAST TIME Apple chairman Steve Jobs appeared in public before resigning as chief executive in late August was not at one of Apple's meticulously choreographed product launches. It took place in the unremarkable chambers of the Cupertino City Council, where Jobs made an unannounced appearance in June to unveil plans for a new, one-building Apple campus, not far from Apple's existing headquarters at One Infinite Loop. Yet in many ways the presentation was quintessential Jobs: He pitched the gargantuan, ring-shaped structure with a mix of flair, theatrics, and hyperbole. "It is a little like a spaceship landed," Jobs said at one point. He later added, "I think we do have a shot at building the best office building in the world." It wasn't long before tech bloggers were buzzing about the iSpaceship.

The campus, if approved and constructed, will house nearly 13,000 employees. Along with the existing headquarters, which has space for 2,800 people and which Apple intends to keep, the iSpaceship will provide plenty of room to grow for years to come. (Apple now has about 12,000 people in Cupertino, the majority of them in a smattering of aging buildings it rents and which it plans to vacate.)

The iSpaceship, a futuristic behemoth enveloped in giant sheets of curved glass, has the elegance and pizzazz of so many other Apple creations. It's also the most visible manifestation that Jobs has been hard at work on what might be his most important product. It is neither an iPhone nor an iPad but rather an enduring and permanent Apple that has the architecture, the processes, the tools—and the soul—to outlive its iconic co-founder. Jobs' legacy as a visionary inventor whose ideas and products reshaped industries is well established. His bigger challenge is to leave behind an institution that carries his DNA and continues to deliver one blockbuster hit after another while pushing the technology industry in new directions, even without Jobs at the helm. If successful it would be his most singular achievement.

The post-Jobs Apple will begin its life at the pinnacle of strength, riding the popularity of the iPhone and iPad, its most successful devices. But the Apple that Jobs created, and the Apple he wants to leave behind, peddles more than mere products. It peddles an elegance and simplicity that pervades everything from products and services (think iTunes) to its stores. "Apple has beautiful artifacts, but what Jobs has been building is a company whose legacy is ideas," says Paul Saffo, the veteran Silicon Valley tech forecaster.

Indeed, Apple's gadgets are far more than a collection of great products. They are an ecosystem of related devices that are ushering in a new era of computing. Until recently, however, that ecosystem was incomplete. Jobs sought to add the missing piece in June when he introduced iCloud, a set of online services designed to tie all of Apple's products together and make it easier for millions of people to access music, photos, files, and software across devices.

It would be easy to dismiss iCloud as little more than a set of useful software tools. Jobs doesn't see it that way. He sees it as a fundamental piece of Apple's future, and to make it a reality, he has built one of the world's largest data centers—the size of nine football fields—which opened recently in Maiden, N.C. With a price tag that will reach $1 billion, the building is indicative of iCloud's central role in extending Apple's franchise. It also is the physical embodiment of a culture of cannibalization that Jobs has lived by and that he no doubt wants to embed into a post-Jobs Apple. "We are going to demote the PC and the Mac to just be a device," Jobs said when he unveiled iCloud. "We are going to move the digital hub, the center of your digital life, into the cloud." Jobs first established his legacy by helping create the PC era in the 1980s. Now he's unsentimentally closing out that chapter to extend both his legacy and Apple's central role in a new post-PC, post-Jobs era.

The plan, like so many of Jobs' moves, could seem almost foolhardy at first blush. When Jobs opened Apple's first store in Tysons Corner, Va., the company's foray into retailing was met with skepticism and even scorn. Ten years and more than 345 stores later, Apple has become one of the most admired retailers in the world. Jobs' decision has become a teachable moment. Literally. A team of business professors hired by Apple has written case studies about the stores and other major Apple moves. They are taught internally by top executives to more-junior managers and are meant to serve as a reference for future generations of Apple leaders. Called Apple University, it was inspired by a similar program at Pixar, the animation studio Jobs sold to Disney. Top leaders, meanwhile, attend secret annual retreats where they absorb the Jobs Way. He discusses products, vision, and strategy. "Steve has always approached everything with the same energy and detail," said Regis McKenna, a marketing guru who worked with Jobs in the 1980s. "He's taken the same attitude he has toward products and design and applied it to management."

Even as Jobs has been working to imprint Apple with his vision, he has been cementing his personal legacy. For the past 18 months Jobs has cooperated with Walter Isaacson, the former managing editor of *Time*, who is writing his bi-

PREVIOUS SPREAD: TRUNK ARCHIVE

A RENDERING OF APPLE'S PROPOSED HEADQUARTERS, DUBBED iSPACESHIP, BY FOSTER & PARTNERS

CITY OF CUPERTINO

ography. While Jobs is said to have no editorial control over the book, which comes out in November, it will be the first authorized biography of Jobs. It suggests an effort by Jobs to tell the official story of his life—and as such will probably serve as an instruction manual on Jobsian culture: It is sure to be important reading for future Apple employees.

Jobs, of course, was not about to hand off his most important product—Apple itself—lightly. Twice before he put Tim Cook, his trusted lieutenant, to the test. Both times Cook performed as well as anyone could have expected. In January, Jobs went on medical leave for the third time. He retained the CEO title and once again put Cook in charge, and during this most recent "interim" period Apple's lead in tablets grew, its phone business accelerated, and the company briefly became the most valued in America, surpassing Exxon Mobil.

Jobs began to consider his resignation in earnest in late July, according to people who know him, after he realized that he would not be able to go back to Apple full-time. These people say that Jobs suffers ups and downs. Some days he is able to hold meetings and weigh in on decisions. Some days he remains housebound and cancels appointments. While he could have chosen the status quo—remaining CEO, with Cook leading day-to-day operations—Jobs decided to take the next step in the transition. On Aug. 24, he went to Apple headquarters for an emotional board meeting, where he made his resignation official. Apple announced the news later in the day.

The people who know him say that little will change at Apple for now—as long as Jobs' health doesn't take a turn for the worse. As chairman, Jobs will stay involved in the things he likes—fine-tuning products, for example—much as he has since January. But the transition to a post-Jobs Apple, precipitated by Jobs' failing health, will have moved further along. Apple will have taken one more gradual step in a smooth and orderly succession that Jobs planned so as to lessen the shock on employees and investors.

It will take years to find out whether Jobs has succeeded in creating a company that can not only outlive him but also continue to be a formidable innovation pacesetter. There are plenty who believe that without Jobs, some of Apple's magic will be lost. "We know less about this than we'd like," says Nancy F. Koehn, a historian at the Harvard Business School. (Apple is known for its secrecy and declined to comment for this story.) Koehn said Jobs had an unmatched set of skills that include vision, intuition, creativity, and leadership. "There is no evidence that any of these has been institutionalized," she says. "If Steve has a great intuition about what consumers want, how is the company without Steve going to know what consumers want?"

Jobs, for his part, says the post-Jobs Apple is ready for primetime. "I believe Apple's brightest and most innovative days are ahead of it," he wrote in his resignation letter. And some in the outside world appear to agree. Despite talk that Apple may never be the same, the company's shares barely budged. It seems that Wall Street, at least, took one look at the post-Jobs Apple and decided it liked what it saw.

107

STEVIE WONDER
BY THE NUMBERS
BY ANNE VANDERMEY

STEVE JOBS' PRODUCT PRESENTATIONS
(RIGHT) WERE ROCK STAR EVENTS
THAT CONTINUALLY DISRUPTED THE
INDUSTRY. HERE ARE A FEW OF OUR
FAVORITE FACTS ABOUT STEVE.

1.7 mb

THE MEMORY OF APPLE'S LISA in 1983—enough
for one or two photos. The PC's price tag?
$10,000. Go, Moore's law.

'i'

WHAT DOES THE "I" STAND FOR in iMac and
iPod? In Steve's iMac introduction in
1998, he said the "i" stands for "Internet,
individual, instruct, inform, inspire."

$10 million

WHAT JOBS PAID DIRECTOR GEORGE LUCAS to buy
Pixar in 1986. Twenty years later Jobs sold the
movie company to Disney for $7.4 billion.
Today Jobs owns 7.4% of the entertainment
giant, worth roughly $4.5 billion, or more
than twice his Apple stake.

$4,032

REVENUE PER SQUARE FOOT five years after the
first Apple store opened in 2001. The next best
that year? Tiffany, with $2,666.

1976: APPLE I WITH STEVE WOZNIAK

1977: APPLE II

1979: APPLE II

1990: NEXT

1993: NEXT

1998: iMAC

1999: POWER MAC G4

1999: iMOVIE

2000: POWER MAC G4 CUBE

2002: FLAT-PANEL iMAC

2002: APPLE STORE, SOHO

2003: *FINDING NEMO*

2004: OS X TIGER

2004: U2 iPOD

2005: MAC MINI

2006: iPOD SHUFFLE

2007: iPOD NANO

2007: iPHONE

2010: iADS

2010: iPOD NANO

2010: APP STORE

1981: APPLE II
1983: LISA
1984: MACINTOSH
1988: NEXT
1988: NEXT

1999: iBOOK
1999: iMAC
1999: OS 9
1999: POWERBOOK G3
1999: PIXAR'S TOY STORY 2

2001: TITANIUM POWERBOOK
2001: APPLE STORE WITH TIM COOK
2001: OS X
2001: iBOOK
2001: iPOD/iTUNES

2003: POWERBOOK G4
2003: POWER MAC G5
2004: iPOD MINI
2004: iLIFE
2004: 30" CINEMA DISPLAY

2005: ROKR PHONE
2005: iPOD NANO
2005: VIDEO iPOD
2006: 5TH AVENUE STORE
2006: APPLE TV

2008: MACBOOK AIR
2008: iPHONE SOFTWARE DEVELOPMENT KIT
2008: iPOD NANO
2010: iPAD
2010: iPHONE 4

2010: APPLE TV
2011: iPAD 2
2011: iCLOUD

Chapter Five

Fortune
September 26, 2011

PHOTO CREDITS FOR STEVIE WONDER: BY THE NUMBERS ON PAGE 112

THANKS, STEVE. WE'VE ALL BEEN LUCKY TO LIVE IN A WORLD WHERE THERE WAS A PERSON WITH SUCH AN IMAGINATION. BY STANLEY BING

I WANT TO TAKE THIS OPPORTUNITY, before time and our common mortality rob me of the chance to do so, to thank you, Steve Jobs, for all that you have done for me. No, I never had the privilege of meeting you, or had a chance to get yelled at by you in a business meeting, or even watch your charisma transform an audience into acolytes. But I feel as if I know you well enough to express, as you ascend to your new role as chairman, the sadness I feel and my gratitude for so many of the good things that you have brought to my life. It's not business. It's personal.

I want to thank you for my graphical interface. There were computers, of course, before you made that first Mac. They could run only one program at a time. They had no graphics. You knew that was lame. You imagined the alternative—multiple programs, launched by clicks, running concurrently in a windowed field. Last night I watched a movie, printed photos, harvested e-mail, and bought a bunch of business socks, all at the same time. So thanks for my GUI.

I want to thank you for my mouse. Can you imagine a world without mouses? I can't. Before you bred them for commercial use, a person needed a host of keyboard commands to get anything done, and a lot of programming code to produce words and numbers on paper. I read somewhere that you got the vision after you visited Xerox's PARC. They showed you what they were up to, but they sort of didn't know what they had. You ran with it. Because that's the way you did everything. All in. Feet first.

I want to thank you for all Macs, great and small. I went to your Apple Store the other day and saw a tidy row of new machines, from the slender new Airs to the massive towers of power. I wanted every one. They're pretty and shiny, unlike my big old black rubberized clunker the corporation gave me, and

the last time I got a virus was just before I put my Windows PC into the closet. That was when I sent the phrase "I love you" to 22,000 fellow employees and the CEO. "I love you too, Bing, but let's not let anybody know," he e-mailed back.

I want to thank you for my Airport Extreme, the small white box through which I get my Internet. Before it, I used to have to plug in and configure this horrible router. It never worked. I often ended up screaming and crying and throwing hardware at the wall. This thing? You just plug it in and use it. Sometimes as I fall asleep I watch the little fellow, with its round eye glowing green in the darkness, a beacon of easy functionality.

Thanks for my iPod, which pretty much defined how I listen to music now. And for iTunes, which you made too easy not to understand. And for my iPad too, which despite all protestations is really nothing more than an Angry Birds machine. No, you can't work on it. So what? Work isn't everything.

And thanks for my new iPhone, which channels a million apps and does everything well except the phone part. A pompous Silicon Valley dude I know used to say, with a weary grin, "Every year is the year for mobile." Until you decided it was, Steve. And so I never have to generate a single unaided thought for the rest of my life. What a relief!

And oh, yeah. Thanks for *Toy Story* too. And *Up*.

Really loved *Up*.

It's been your world, Steve. And we've been lucky enough to run along behind you, picking up goodies as you dropped them in our path. It's a little scary to think that you have gone off to your famous mountaintop and will not return with the next big thing. But at least we can all say we lived in a time when there was a person with such an imagination, and offer thanks in whatever digital or analog format we choose, wherever on earth we may be. We can do that now.

FORTUNE

Managing Editor Andy Serwer
Deputy Managing Editor Hank Gilman
Executive Editor Stephanie Mehta
Design Director Emily Kehe
Director of Photography Mia Diehl
Contributing Editor Brian Dumaine
Copy Chief Carol Gwinn
Designer Anton Ioukhnovets
Photo Editor Armin Harris
Editorial Production Angel Mass
Legal Amy Glickman

Special thanks: Marilyn Adamo, Doris Burke, Maria Carmicino, Rose DeMaria, Michael Myers, Andrea Nasca, Jennifer Reingold, Michael Solita, Rose Unes, Anne VanderMey, Michelle Wolfe

TIME HOME ENTERTAINMENT

Publisher Richard Fraiman
Vice President, Business Development & Strategy Steven Sandonato
Executive Director, Marketing Services Carol Pittard
Executive Director, Retail & Special Sales Tom Mifsud
Executive Director, New Product Development Peter Harper
Director, Bookazine Development & Marketing Laura Adam
Publishing Director Joy Butts
Finance Director Glenn Buonocore
Assistant General Counsel Helen Wan
Assistant Director, Special Sales Ilene Schreider
Book Production Manager Suzanne Janso
Design & Prepress Manager Anne-Michelle Gallero
Associate Book Production Manager Kimberly Marshall

Editorial Director Stephen Koepp

Special thanks: Christine Austin, Jeremy Biloon, Jim Childs, Susan Chodakiewicz, Rose Cirrincione, Jacqueline Fitzgerald, Carrie Hertan, Christine Font, Jenna Goldberg, Lauren Hall, Hillary Hirsch, Mona Li, Amy Mangus, Robert Marasco, Amy Migliaccio, Nina Mistry, Dave Rozzelle, Adriana Tierno, Alex Voznesenskiy, Vanessa Wu

Copyright © 2011 Time Home Entertainment Inc. Published by Fortune Books, an imprint of Time Home Entertainment Inc. • 135 West 50th Street • New York, NY 10020

All rights reserved. No part of this book may be reproduced in any form or by any electronic or mechanical means, including information storage and retrieval systems, without permission in writing from the publisher, except by a reviewer, who may quote brief passages in a review.

All the articles in this book were previously published in substantially the same form in *Fortune* magazine between 1983 and 2011. Some have been edited for length.

Fortune is a registered trademark of Time Inc.

ISBN 13: 978-1-61893-001-9
ISBN 10: 1-61893-001-X
Library of Congress Control Number: 2011940630

We welcome your comments and suggestions about Fortune Books. Please write to us at:
Fortune Books, Attention: Book Editors, P.O. Box 11016, Des Moines, IA 50336-1016.
If you would like to order any of our hardcover Collector's Edition books, please call us at
1-800-327-6388, Monday through Friday, 7 a.m. to 8 p.m., or Saturday, 7 a.m. to 6 p.m.,
Central Time.

PHOTO CREDITS FOR STEVIE WONDER BY THE NUMBERS—FROM LEFT. ROW 1: PAUL SAKUMA—AP, APPLE COMPUTER/AP, RALPH MORSE—TIME LIFE PICTURES/GETTY, TED THAI—TIME LIFE PICTURES/GETTY (2), BERNARD GOTFRYD—GETTY, ED KASHI—VII/CORBIS, DIANA WALKER—SJ/CONTOUR BY GETTY. ROW 2: SARA KRULWICH—THE NEW YORK TIMES/REDUX. AP, MOSHE BRAKHA—AP, PETER MORGAN—REUTERS, ALANG, DE JECACION—GETTY, PAUL SAKUMA—AP, LOUDEMATTES—REUTERS, PETER MORGAN—REUTERS, WIN MCNAMEE—REUTERS, JOHN MABANGLO—AFP/GETTY, JOHN MABANGLO—AFP/GETTY, SUSAN RAGAN—REUTERS. ROW 4: KOICHI KAMOSHIDA—GETTY, MARIO TAMA—GETTY IMAGES, CHRIS POLK—FILMMAGIC/GETTY, ERIKO SUGITA—REUTERS, KIM KULISH—CORBIS, KIM KULISH—CORBIS (2), JUSTIN SULLIVAN—GETTY. ROW 5: JUSTIN SULLIVAN—GETTY, TIM MOSENFELDER—GETTY, MONICA M. DAVEY—EPA/CORBIS, LOUDEMATTES—REUTERS, FREDERIC J. LARSON—THE SAN FRANCISCO CHRONICLE/CORBIS, DAVID BRABYN—CORBIS, KIMBERLY WHITE/BLOOMBERG VIA GETTY, ROW 6: KIMBERLY WHITE/BLOOMBERG VIA GETTY, JUSTIN SULLIVAN—GETTY, JOHN MABANGLO—AFP/GETTY, TONY AVELAR—AFP/GETTY, JUSTIN SULLIVAN—GETTY, JOHN MABANGLO—AFP/GETTY, PAUL MORRIS—REUTERS, ROBERT GALBRAITH—